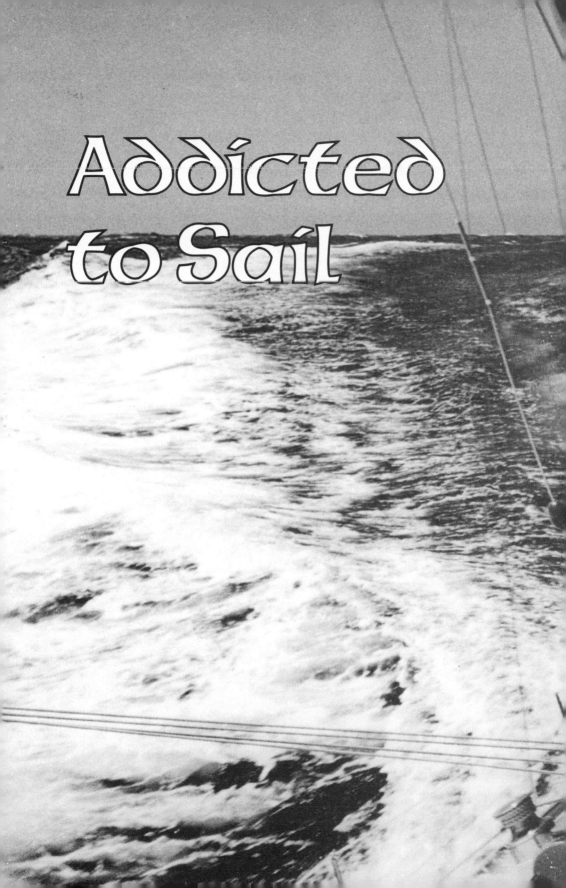

Addicted to Sail

Addicted to Sail

A Half Century of Yachting Experiences

NORRIS D. HOYT

W · W · NORTON & COMPANY

NEW YORK · LONDON

FIRST EDITION

The text of this book is composed in Avanta with display type set in American Uncial Open and Friz Quadrata Bold. Composition and manufacturing by the Haddon Craftsmen. Book design by Marjorie J. Flock.

Library of Congress Cataloging in Publication Data

Hoyt, Norris D.
  Addicted to sail.

  1. Yachts and yachting.   I. Title.
GV813.H695   1987   797.1   86-23620

ISBN 0-393-03316-3

W. W. Norton & Company, Inc., 500 Fifth Avenue, New York, N.Y. 10110
W. W. Norton & Company Ltd., 37 Great Russell Street, London WC1B 3NU

1 2 3 4 5 6 7 8 9 0

Contents

To Kitty— *When Kitty and I took off on our first trans-atlantic voyage together, she was asked by a reporter whether she was frightened. She gave the question serious thought: "No . . . ," she said, "Norris has done it before and he likes it." Five transatlantics later and after a particularly rough passage from Newport to St. Thomas, she remarked that passagemaking was like having a baby, the sense of accomplishment was greater than the pangs. Both statements are true. It's much harder to be the cook, the reserve helmsman, the consultant for all my doubts and problems, the balance wheel for the crew, and the warning voice of caution than it is to be the skipper, the mere administrator.*

Now that I've retired from most ocean racing, and am cruising full time with her, I realize that I've made the reward squadron, out of the heat of the battle and into all the joys of sailing with the perfect mate.

Addicted
to Sail

1

Considerably Larger Than Life

J. P. MORGAN, who in some ways wasn't exactly your common garden variety sailing chap, is said to have been "willing to do business with anybody, but to sail only with gentlemen." Ignorant authors have made much of "cabin fever" and the extent to which the close quarters, long hours, and stresses of wind and weather develop animosities on lengthy voyages. Yet I've sailed twenty-three times across the Atlantic, and I've been delighted, at the end of every trip, with every member of every crew. Irving and Exy Johnson sailed the world with strangers for fifty years, and ended up with thousands of friends. Actually, the physical intimacy of sailing, and the close-up exposure to new people, or to new sides of old acquaintances, is exploration as fascinating as that of the foreign ports one reaches. I suspect that people who did business with old J. P. were reasonably unwilling to go along with him, and that people aboard his yacht made desperate efforts to be agreeable. What splendid explorations of character he must have missed!

For one thing, as the days lengthen into weeks at sea, you achieve a sense of such great intimacy that you let loose the less conscious aspects of your own personality, and enjoy reciprocal displays. Imagine, for instance, the horseplay that got my old friend and frequent transatlantic companion the nickname of "The Human Salad." *Ticonderoga* had a midship's hatch with a large flap on each side which opened with hand cranks. "The Human Salad," sunbathing nude on deck, was

Grosmiller, "the human salad," sails and plays sweet music.

Grosmiller, in mid-Atlantic, adjusts the spinnaker the casual way.

captured by the crew below as he dropped through one flap. They ground the flap down around him and decorated his extruding portions with pressure cans of whipped cream and various festive greens. Thus suitably attired, like Adam after the Fall, he provided a temporary centerpiece. Not your home decor.

On another passage, the boat becalmed for three days off the Shetlands, I watched the vice-president of DuPont in charge of R. and D. restlessly and completely disassemble the diesel engine, install all new gaskets, and reassemble the engine so that it ran, I guess, just as well as if he'd left it alone. His faith in people wasn't as great as his faith in his own mechanical aptitude, however, and he had hacksawed off the faucets in the ship's enclosed head, plugged them with wood, and had made a teak enclosure in the galley for a gallon bottle. Each gallon of water we used had to be recorded on a pad attached to the enclosure. We had 150 gallons for eight of us, for, as it turned out, eighteen days, and, after the agonizing hours we spent drifting across the finish line (our hard blow died too soon), there was enough water left for a shower for everyone but the helmsman, me. I can forgive Hank his estimate of our characters; he'd probably read books about people sneaking water and eating each other in the terminal stages of shipwreck.

Shipwreck has happened, of course, but there is an irony to it. The people who are shipwrecked are not wealthy, well-equipped ocean racers with thousands of miles of experience. That particular lot never shipwrecks, never writes books about how to avoid shipwreck, and never crosses oceans in ancient crocks that are terminally ill with rot, rust, and shipworm. Whales never attack the well endowed. Gales avoid coupon clippers. Hurricanes harass hackers. The other side of the coin, of course, is that the repetitively successful never get to write a book about their ordeal. Ordealwise, less is more.

But I digress (it's a habit I love). Let me recall a marvelous passage from Newfoundland to Falmouth, England, on *Figaro* (apart from one gale, that is, in which waves swept over the cockpit and the duty helmsman). Our skipper, Bill Snaith, industrial designer, author, artist, actor, architect, and shameless intriguer with the truth, had just redis- covered *The Pickwick Papers*. Bill could do all the accents: Oxcam,

London Cockney, Lancs, Hants, Herts, Scottish, Irish, etc. *Pickwick* got him where he lived, and each evening he did a full chapter for us aloud, outdickensing Dickens, as we sipped the evening drink (one). His sons, Cloudy, Skip, and Jocko, the most entertained of us all, had never been read to by the old man at home.

On the Fourth of July we decorated the cabin with balloons and streamers, wore funny hats, had wine with dinner, and Bill treated us to an appropriate patriotic oration: "Fellow Americans, we sail yet again to do battle with the Dastardly British. . . . We have long paid feet of tribute and yards of genoa to the arbitrary RORC rating law . . ." He had us cheering, and the kids rolling. His previous orations at home had concerned misdeeds.

During the final chapter of *Pickwick*, we blew smartly down the Channel, thinking, at 1700 GMT (Zulu), of Cowes by morning. Off Falmouth, Jocko entered strenuous objection. "Do you want me to starve, Pop?" he agonized. "We've been out of peanut butter for two days!" Bill, an understanding gourmet, agreeably put in to a mooring at Falmouth (our anchors were buried) and took us all to a restaurant. Jocko, shockingly, ordered steak instead of peanut butter, and wolfed it down with gusto. During the meal, a gale blew up, we couldn't get out to the boat, and two yachts were sunk in the Channel, drowning a famous pathologist. Our lives had been saved by peanut butter, The American Way.

Passagemaking is not without tensions, however. I remember one Transatlantic Race with a dear friend, Curtis Bok, judge, author, and patron of music. He had had a "massive myocardiac infarct" (as I remember), but he saw no reason to let this interrupt the flow of his experience. We had cruised to England together two years before, and he'd learned to love the endless horizons, the passing of time ritualized into watches, and the company of fellow enthusiasts who weren't angling for donations. His close friend, and doctor, Stroud, a nonsailor, had advised strongly against a Transatlantic Race. If we were going across, however, I saw racing as a precautionary measure—we'd have more attention on us if Curtis's heart became whimsical. We also shipped my college roommate, Bill Lee, who had recently had, and recovered from, heart trouble. *Alphard* was a thirty-eight-foot ketch,

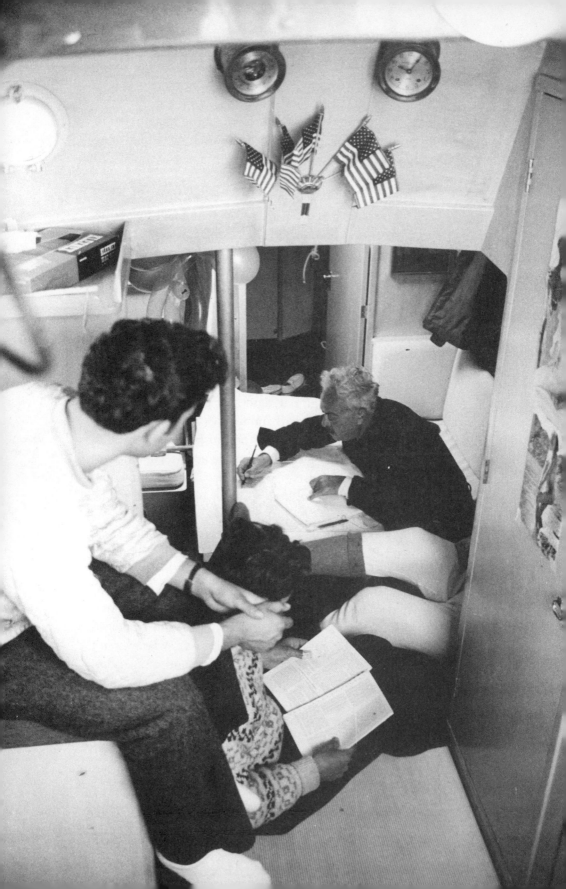

Navigator Curtis Bok—race to Spain.

Before the 4th of July dinner, Snaith plots our position—Figaro III.

tender enough to develop barnacles in the cockpit seats after several
days on the wind, but quite quick off it. To make sure our pace was
conservative, my wife Kitty came along as cook. The coal stove was next
to the companionway, the fridge across the way; both thus exposed the
cook to spray and whatever washed aboard. We started from Newport,
Rhode Island, and the fleet rapidly disappeared ahead over the horizon.
We were the smallest boat, and had about a two-day handicap in a
twenty-day race.

Redwood Wright, currently head of Bermuda Biological, and Ted
Robbins completed the crew. Curtis tired readily, and we were more
than attentive to his condition, easing the boat off when a more weath-
erly course would have been rougher, and even heaving to to bake a
cake and have a pleasant meal. We hove to, comfortably again, during
a full two-day gale outside the Bay of Biscay, and had a vigorous second
evening. The water in the cockpit seats got to the wiring under them,
and the ship's horn shorted and began to blow deafeningly. Redwood,
very large and very quick, opened the lockers and pulled out wires by
the handful, thus eliminating horn, pumps, motor, and lighting. The
gale died, we drifted under spinnaker, mizzen staysail, and mainsail,
and eventually finished last, rewiring the vessel the while. At the finish
line there was an enormous bunch of calla lilies, and later a silver
trophy, which was presented to Kitty, the only girl in the race, as "Cook
on the Last Boat to Finish." Actually, we had been only twelve hours
out of the corrected time money! Ashore Curtis, shaggy in tweeds and
twenty days worth of hair, was in tears reading a telegram. Doctor
Stroud had died, Philadelphia being a greater strain than the Atlantic
Ocean.

The strain in racing, heart attacks aside, is largely borne by the
skipper, who is understandably considerably larger than life in his
directives. Different skippers use different techniques to maintain as-
cendancy over their crews—Huey Long playing, hour by hour, the
intense drama of his life; Dick Nye treating the worst that can happen
as no more than the routine of a farmer's day. When we won a
Transatlantic Race on the fifty-three-foot *Ondine III*, they had shortened the mast by eight feet and cut down the sails appropriately. The
weather, after the start in Newport and for five days, was mild ahead,

hazy, and frustrating, and we dropped steadily behind. Huey raged around the boat, insisting on a new sail every half hour, seating to weather on the aluminum deck all hands not sail-handling or steering. The boat labored against the Labrador Current, which froze us to our bellybuttons. Then minor goof-up in changing the genoas brought on tragedy: "There goes the ball game!" he intoned, shoulders slumped in despair, his face the mask of tragedy.

Inevitably, the wind that had been waiting in the wings came on, howling at forty knots. Gradually it swung from northeast around to southwest, and the moment the indicators in the navigator's salon, protected from the blast, indicated wind abeam, Huey was in the companionway, elated. "The wind's abeam! Set the spinnaker!" We looked at him in wonder. "Set the spinnaker? It's blowing forty! Go up on the foredeck—your ears will blow into your mouth!" He put on the face of angry Jove. "I am the captain! Set the spinnaker!" We had a six-ounce spinnaker, triple-stitched, and the main was, of course, deeply reefed. But we set it. Broaching now and then, we had three days of 248 miles, 235 miles, and 234 miles, surfing hundreds of yards at a time. And through all this hair-raising excitement, Huey whacked the boat on the side of the hull and cried, in love again, "Come on, you big baby-blue beauty! Go! Go!"

Nye's technique was quite the opposite. A stocky figure, he conceals a mind of devious whimsicality behind the rubicund face and noncommittal manner of a surly farmer. In the midst of hail and gale, the ship reeling, he'd rouse out the other watch with the ironic admonition, "All right; hit the deck; this is what you came for!" The 1957 Fastnet, with a higher percentage of experienced sailors in it than the '79 disaster, was started in a gale, sailed in a gale, and finished in a gale. Out of some 130 entries, only half started and only seven finished. Neither lives nor boats were lost. Nye's *Carina* was first around the Rock, first to finish, and winner of the race for the third successive time. Her repair bill equaled her cost.

Going out the Solent, off the Needles, when the first great seas began smashing the fleet, frames broke, and by the time a passage inside the Shambles and in the lee of Portland Bill was negotiated, *Carina* had an exploded bilge stringer, a split main keel brace, and enough leaks to keep two pumps going. Nye, off watch, lay dozing belly up in his bunk, a clenched cigar in his mouth's corner. Agitated, a crew member shook him to attention: "Dick, the bilge stringer's gone, and the planks forward squirt down when we go up and up when we go down. Just take a look!" Nye gave him the evil eye. "Why should I look? I'm not a carpenter."

Thus encouraged, they pressed on, rounded the Fastnet first, and blew out the first of three spinnakers. Nye's instructions were, "Set the next bag, what the hell, it's paid for." As they finished he summed up the entire race, "We're over; let the damn thing sink." Actually, with two pumps going and a third slave bailing into the head and pumping, the boat survived to be rebuilt and take second in the next Fastnet.

That time I'd been invited to cruise over and race by Nye in his casual mode. "You'll enjoy it Norry; drinks every night, no light sails, just cruising." Naturally, rounding the bell off Newport's Brenton Reef, he informed us, "Rod Stephens cruises at 90 percent of racing efficiency, let's get some sail on this bucket." We crossed the Atlantic (St. John's, Newfoundland, to Round Island in the Scillies) in ten days, five hours, through five days of fog with intermittent icebergs. We carried the spinnaker.

Our first stop was Plymouth, where, unfortunately, I was acquainted with two splendid British Eccentrics—the owner of the Plymouth Wineries and her managing director, Britain's last man off the beach at Dunkirk. He couldn't possibly be more Guards mustachioed, pin-striped, flare-lapelled, home, Britain, and The Flag. She is lavender and old lace, shy, slightly batty, and given to impressionistic creations with gauze, paper, and *objets trouvés*.

Our anchor was barely down (my mother had written ahead), when a mission came aboard, a young officer complete with a sword that involved itself with the companionway. He invited us to drinks at the naval mess, and delivered an engraved invitation to a reception at the winery for "The American Yacht *Carina* and Crew." The welcoming committee included the Lord Mayor, a scattering of local nobility, and,

Cory Cramer navigates; Skipper Nye dresses informally.

of course, the lot from the winery. They had previously sponsored the *Mayflower* reproduction, and replayed the same party, complete with nubile young ladies in low-cut, square-bosomed, rather un-Puritan costumes. The key point of the decor was one of Milady's impressionistic creations, vaguely symbolizing Yachting.

Nye put on his surly farmer mode. "Christ, Norry," he gruffly shouted, "why'd you get me into this zoo?" "Wait till you hear the toasts," I encouraged him. "Toasts? Am I gonna have to talk?" "Ummmm," I brilliantly replied. "Well, I'm not," he declared, squinting at me to judge the impact, "You're the mouth of Newport—you do it." I knew he didn't mean it. He loves a gallery, talks as though his ideas have just now come to him, and has a flawless sense of audience and timing. Also, at base, he is wicked. The toasts, when they came, were as anticipated, leaning on hands across the sea, a heritage of island blood, seafaring nations, partners in democracy, and so forth. After this too sufficient flattery, there was rather too long a silence, in which Nye looked significantly at me. I made a small move forward. "Wait a minute," he said, stepping in front of the Creation and into the spotlight, "We didn't come here for hands across the sea, or any of that baloney," he dropped the bomb, paused. Faces fell; silence reigned; people shuffled uneasily. "We're just run-of-the-mill guys who like sailing." Another hideous pause. Nye smiled a fat, delighted smile, stopped looking at his feet, spread his arms, and went on, "We sailed here because here's the best race in the world against the best racers in the world, and it's sails across the sea, not hands. We love it here and we'll come again and again, as often as you'll let us." Nothing gets more applause than relief; and as it thundered out, the miserable wretch winked at me, stuck his cigar back in his face, and began conning our dotty hostess. A summer with Nye was uplifting.

In essence, the slow exploration and appreciation of personality is one of the great bonuses of cruising. It comes from realizing how complex, fascinating, and wholly different from everyone else each person is. That's why shipmates, roommates, brothers, and wives are classics in our libraries of recollections, and for each, some small tale remembered recalls the whole, rich volume. You love them for who they are, not what they've done, have, or can do. My friend Tom

Clagett is a protean personality whose company is endlessly unexpected. He varies from pure Southern mushball corn to showing the single-minded brutality of an attacking rhino. He has a very good mind, busy as an eggbeater with his own or anyone else's business; he loves small details, and is as delighted as a child with surprises and discoveries. His intense pride in his skills is only equaled by his complete lack of it when you least expect it. We've had some great days together, his boat or mine.

We were cruising the Dalmatian Coast together, on a fifty-foot Angus Primrose designed single-hander, built for my friend Guy Goodbody and lent to us for my sabbatical. Clagett had arrived from Washington twenty-three hours after my telephone call, and had a grand time shopping the flea market in Split—emerging with (1) a plastic razor-comb for trimming the hair of dogs or people, and (2) a metal thing that enabled one to extract from a potato an endless curl that was round in section, resulting in french-fried end products that looked like worms and left half the potato for down-the-road uses.

Later, in Italy, he dug shells shamelessly from someone else's sandstone blocks to have them carbon-dated at the Smithsonian. A connoisseur of booze, he located a bottle of *Vecchio Romano*, a lethal brandy. Goodbody had long since joined us, and since he was the owner of the boat, he and I went through the ritual of offering each other the helm for dockings. In Hvar, after a splendid, vinous dinner, we drank the brandy slowly, and were gazing at both moons when Clagett erupted, tears in his tone, "You know what you bastards have been doing? You've never let me dock the boat." I'd long known that he could maneuver anything from a catboat to an aircraft carrier with total precision, and belatedly realized that it was one of his things. Thereafter we had a three-way ritual.

I wrote up my favorite Clagett story in a sail article about our Yugoslavian cruise. As wealthy yacht owners, accompanied from port to port by Goodbody's new Jaguar, our tourism was unfortunately encouraged by lower prices on gasoline, booze, and exchange. The discrepancy did not make us popular with the less-privileged natives. Our lack of fluency, or even vocabulary, in Serbo-Croatian was also a handicap when we wanted to buy eggs. All six feet seven inches of

Clagett, six feet two inches of Goodbody (peering from under prehensile eyebrows), and the bulk of me approached a table of local sailors, who were drinking wine and chatting. We tried "eier?" "huevos?" "oeufs?" "eggs?," without result. They gazed coldly at us, as though we were trying to borrow money. Suddenly Clagett stooped, cackled like a hen from his squat, and produced his hands cradling an egg shape from under his crotch. In instant recognition, they rose from the table, roaring with laughter, hugged him, poured us wine, seated us all, and went back to helpless laughter. When the bottle was empty, we rose, and they led us down the street to a small house where, perforce following instructions from our guides, Clagett did a repeat performance, adding a few ruffles and flourishes to the cock-a-doodle doings. The lady of the house collapsed into her apron with giggles, led us to the back yard, pressed eggs and vegetables in profusion upon us, pausing now and then to giggle a few more stanzas into her apron. Thus supplied, we went back to the square and Clagett bought other bottles. From resentment, friendship came from one master stroke. It made a splendid and moral end to my story, which was, in due time, published.

Shortly thereafter, I had a telephone call from Clagett in Washington. "You crazy bastard," he yelled. "Do you know what you've done to me?!" I didn't make the connection; I had no idea. "I came into the Explorers Club for a drink and lunch, and everyone at the bar made rooster noises at me!"

He loved it. Such joyous memories as these I cherish as the best part of the sailing life. You really get to know great people, even better perhaps than their families or their secretaries can. This book celebrates such memories.

2

The Second
Second-Happiest Day

IF A SAILOR'S second-happiest day is when he buys his first boat, and his happiest day is when he sells it, I'm sure my happiest day was when I sold my first boat *and* bought my second! That great day signaled both the culmination of a love affair and the routing of a massed front of prophets of doom. It all went way back.

From my time in the fourth grade to 1930, we lived in Morris Cove, inside the breakwaters of New Haven Harbor and over near Lighthouse Point. We lived three blocks from the water and three blocks from the swamp, and I don't know which gave me more pleasure —messing around the swamp (which then had a clear brook down its middle, flowing over watercress), or going sailing with our next-door neighbor, a bearded rebel in a day when mankind was clean-jawed. He neglected his wife for his catboat. His wife loved neglect. In conversation she called her husband "Mr. Munson (Caleb)." She was a valiant housekeeper, a redoubtable cook, and a friend (part-time) of every child in the neighborhood. Blonde, mild, small, and comfortably female, she couldn't have been nicer. We loved her. She kept an upper drawer in the kitchen full of balloons, and, if you called on her, you got either cookies, doughnuts, or a balloon.

I think, at this distance, that her husband had a reasonable un-earned income, because he spent lots of time around the house, painting, fussing, silhouetting all his tools above his workbench, and consulting with other husbands about repairs to domestic disasters. He also spent lots of time, head down, in the bowels of his Reo Flying-Cloud truck. The forerunner of the station wagon, it had a roof over the wood-paneled long-body, supported by vertical wood uprights braced with metal castings. The roof extended forward into a curved-down hat brim over a two-part windshield, and the spare tires were in wells on the front fenders. It creaked like a boat when we tacked around corners. The daily vegetable man had almost the same thing.

The catboat wintered on a stretch of paved road end that ran into the beach next to the Wehles' (they owned the local brewery); it was wrapped in heavy canvas tied to the ground with steel stakes. After Easter vacation, Mr. Munson (Caleb) spent afternoons on the catboat, either inside with the one-lunger, or outside with paint and varnish. By late May he was ready to regild his wife's name (Minnie-Louise) on the boat's bright mahogany transom. The rudder was retrieved from a wet-wrap under canvas. When it had swelled out all its shrink-gaps and dried for a couple of hours in the sun, it got painted on both sides with red bottom paint. With several of us getting in the way (helping), Mr. Munson (Caleb) horsed it over the pintles, hung it, and we were ready for the launch.

At low tide on a Saturday, planks were aligned on the beach, the boat's rollers were unblocked, tackles were attached to her two skids and connected to long iron stakes driven into the low water line of the beach. The stakes angled out to sea. A new roller from his garage was positioned behind the skids. With six kids on one tackle and Mr. Munson on the other, the *Minnie-Louise* rocked and creaked her way down the beach, Mr. Munson admonishing us with "Harder!" and "Ease off, sailors!" as she veered out of line.

Five hours later, give or take an hour, the helpers and a few extra hands were waiting—shoes and stockings off and plus fours rolled above the knees—as the tide began to lift her stern. "O.K.! Sailors, shove!" was the command, and screeching at the icy water, we rushed onto the cradle and pushed valiantly until the *Minnie-Louise* bobbed bravely into New Haven Harbor. Her mooring was about 100 yards offshore, under the guns and shelter of the headland that held Fort Hale. Mr. Munson (Caleb) motored to it and spent the evening pumping, running rigging, bending on sail, and generally messing around. We abandoned the beach and drifted home. I stopped off at the Munson's to tell Mrs. Munson (Minnie-Louise) that the boat was successfully launched. After a launching, she always said, "Oh dear! Mr. Munson (Caleb) won't be home tonight!" Generally, "Fat" Allo came along with me to the Munsons to absorb whatever was offered. In general, I hoped for balloons rather than food.

All the women my mother knew in Morris Cove disapproved of Mr. Munson. His idleness was an offense to the Congregational work ethic; his wife's placid docility in the face of visible neglect ("He treats That Boat better than Minnie-Louise") an outrage to domestic example, and the Munsons' obvious satisfaction in their deviant pattern the cruelest cut of all. Worse still, the neighborhood's children always behaved with grace and polity when scarfing up Mrs. Munson's bounty, and she assiduously praised us to our parents (who had to accept us as we *really* were, all 365 days [and nights] of the year). Since there was no release for the full reservoir of neighborhood resentment, (everyone was "on Minnie-Louise's side"), it disbursed itself in criticism of the catboat, boating in general, and any male's connection with it.

In my mother's mind, "That Boat" was thus imprinted as a symbol of male injustice, willful intransigence, and needless expense. Worse still, Mr. Munson (Caleb) used to take me sailing when I couldn't swim a stroke, and the awful risk gave my mother the fantods. He always wrapped me in one of those ancient, white, overstuffed kapok life vests, so that I looked like a sausage on toothpicks. We'd beat out to Lighthouse Point beach, to the beacon off Branford, and then we'd sail through the islands, boom against the shrouds. Beating out was my favorite—*Minnie-Louise* heeled about twenty-five degrees, and I'd be up to windward on the rail, several times my height above the waves. My mother occasionally met us as we rowed ashore, having watched my oblate silhouette perched opposite the boom, ready to be swept away. Mother never trusted sail, anyway, not since she had crewed summers for her gigantic brothers, Frank and Will, in a half-rater on Lake Massawippi at North Hatley, Canada, and had been frequently capsized while jibing in a squall.

So much for background. I'll pass over the formative years of school and college, when I ceased to be a constant problem (attending in turn three schools) and became an overperformer (earning honors, world records in swimming, and a Ph.D.). Outside New Haven, we rented boats at Stony Creek and took girls sailing; I ocean raced with Frank Bissell on *Dorothy Q.* I got married. One year into my second job— teaching Chaucer, Milton, and Nineteenth-Century Poetry at Clark University—two wonderful things happened. We bought our first boat, and Kitty became pregnant. Somehow, we'd managed to get $1,500 ahead of expenditures. Kitty had painted a few portraits, and I was doing rewrite for a women's magazine on the side. Also, I'd signed on for a summer job in New Haven as Assistant to the Director of the Committee on Cultural Relations with Latin America (CCRLA). Re-writing translations and selling them to North American magazines, I usually managed to outrage my seven translators. The authors were delighted with the fees and never protested.

Kitty and I had a wonderful month of buying the boat. John Killam Murphy, from whom my parents rented our summer house on Killam's Point, was a yacht broker and catboat owner *(Tabby).* He'd even bought his children two Wee Scots. Mother liked him since he was older than she was and charming. But she was a bit sniffy about his "doing nothing but renting cottages and selling boats," and she totally disapproved of his supplying his children with "an expensive way to waste time."

John K. Murphy had a great eye for a pretty girl, and Kitty en-chanted him. When, on his advice, we wanted to go boat searching for "a good, sound hull that needs cosmetic attention," he offered to spend as many weekends as we needed if we covered gasoline and board. We together found *Hardtack*, in East Boothbay, Maine, a twenty-five-foot sloop designed and built by Jack Stevens of Goudy and Stevens for himself. She came well supplied with tableware, insurance, a genoa, a whisker pole, and a Universal Bluejacket Twin, all for $1800. Using a bit of advanced salary, we owned her, and sailed her down from Maine in eight days, three of which were spent, galebound, in York Harbor, Maine, correcting finals and telephoning in the grades. We had a great summer of weekend cruising (criticized by mother as "extravagant")

Hardtack, *our first boat, 1940.*

and announced the pregnancy at Thanksgiving. Cheers and congratulations, combined with "That Boat" misgivings. I'm sure mother was asking herself where she had failed.

But winning the battle isn't winning the campaign. In our second summer of ownership, sailing was restricted to Long Island Sound (the Dead Sea), Kitty had Katy, and John Killam Murphy resigned his commission as Reserve Commander and was reprocured as Lt. Jr. Grade to become Captain of the Port of New Haven. In a mother-hen way, Mom underlined the fact that my responsibilities were greater. She then rounded up an offer of $2,500 for the boat, which had outsailed some larger local boats. I had contracted for a second summer ·vith the CCRLA, our time was limited, etc. The gist of her message was, "Now is the time . . ."

For the previous winter, *Hardtack* had lived in Seth Persson's yard, where he later built *Finisterre*. Seth, superb boatbuilder that he was, had been drafted from his war job of building troop-carrying gliders at the Ivoryton Piano Works and sent to India as a metalworker. There he spent the duration, handmaking officer's cigarette lighters. His father, Frans, ran the yard and encouraged everyone to do his own work. We were his poorest yacht owners and his favorite charity. Since we lived aboard the boat during spring vacation while we sanded and painted, we brought the food, and he cooked all our meals and served them in his house. This, of course, gave him the long evenings to chat Kitty up with "moving tales of field and flood" about his youth spent before the mast.

But, and here's the kernel of the matter, I had fallen in love again. The boat next to *Hardtack* was *Wagtail*, an exquisite thirty-two-foot Rhodes cutter, double-ended. She was French gray, with red boot top, red cove-molding, and red name, the latter carved, with her hailing port, Lyme, Connecticut, in incised romans. Her trim was white; her interior was paneled in waxed butternut. She had a coal stove whose doors opened so you could watch the flames, had won her class in Off-Soundings in 1937, and had a four-cylinder Gray that ran like a watch. Her owner, an architect, had built her in his backyard under the instructive supervision of John Ely, retired boatbuilder, of Ely's Landing, on the Connecticut River. Her inch-and-a-quarter cedar planks hadn't a single butt joint; her fastenings were hand-forged iron nails clenched over in her oak frames. For a year I'd admired her lovely lines and watched her paint deteriorating. I yearned to do something tender for her.

But faithful to my commitment, I got *Hardtack* into high shine, delivered her to her purchaser, and watched her sail down the Connecticut River and out of sight. Clutching his check, I trudged boatless to our Model A Ford Coupe. Frans leaned on the fender. "Now you happy with no boat? Yah?" he asked. It was all I needed. "Frans, do you suppose Homer K. is home?" "Naw. No chance; he is big architect for Navy; always away." "Well," I said, "Let's call him and see." As fate decided, Homer K. was home, alone, and would love to see me. I had crewed for him twice. He had loved planning and building the boat, but the tension of racing did not enchant him, and his peripatetic responsibilities (he designed naval hospitals) denied him cruising leisure. I poured the full tale of my unrequited passion into his ear, offered him $3,200 for her (anticipating borrowing two months' salary in advance). He ruefully confessed that he'd turned down much more than that a week ago, but he'd disliked the prospective owner who, to beat down the price, had been critical of "amateur building" and "iron fastenings" and "painted trim." "He said it looked like a fishboat . . . I wouldn't have let him have it at any price . . ."

To keep his wife from anguish, Homer K. receipted a bill for "one dollar and other valuable considerations" and I became, as of that moment, the happiest male in Essex, Connecticut.

Driving home, alone, to my wife, my child, my mother, and a full weekend confluence of my three aunts (known as *The Girls*), Uncle Will, and several cousins, I experienced withdrawal symptoms. I rehearsed my mother's litany, beginning with "responsibilities" and "settle down" and proceeding through "expensive toy" to "That Boat." But the blueprints were behind the seat, and the trunk was filled with cleats, lead pigs, and odd bronze gadgets. Homer K. had not only sold the boat, he'd cleaned out his hope chest.

Despite cautious driving, I arrived at the family manse on 39 Clifford Street, across from the Winchester Woods, by five in the afternoon. Uncle Will's Packard, Aunt Jane's Graham-Paige, and my

father's Hupmobile were in the driveway. The screened front porch
buzzed intensely (our whole clan practiced competitive talking). As I
pulled up to the sidewalk, silence fell. Parents, aunts, cousins, my wife,
and my uncle watched my approach. Staring at my feet, I pushed onto
the porch with the rolled blueprints, and expressed my great pleasure
at the company. Mother held off till I veered into aimless conversation
with my cousin Elsie, and then broke in. "Well," she said, "did you
sell the boat?" I uh-huhed. "Did you get the check?" I uh-huhed.
"Well, where is it?"

I bit the bullet. "I haven't got it." Faces fell; Kitty looked ironic;
my father watched the Hartford family in fascination. Their noisy
energy always bemused him. "I bought a bigger boat."

The stricken silence slowly gave way to looks of sympathetic pity
from The Girls to my mother. The cousins gave me their "Boy-Will-
You-Get-It" look, a conditioned reflex from the past. But my mother
was a gallant contender, never downed. After all, I was her First Born,
and the clan needed reminding that Hers had done better than Theirs.
She made an instant attitude adjustment. "Well," she said, "I hope it
was a real bargain!" I unrolled the blueprints for admiration.

By the time summer was in flower, I had been commissioned in
the U. S. Navy and was under training at Ft. Schuyler. Weekends, I
managed to escape to Killam's Point and take folks sailing, often
mother and The Girls. In the drifting air prevalent off Branford, gas
rationing being in force, they even played bridge in the cockpit, and
between hands, mother would wax philosophical, "Norris" she'd say,
"this yacht certainly is a bargain." Down memory lane with Mr. Munson (Caleb), "That Boat" had been retired forever.

3

All Hail the O.P.B.C.

UNFORTUNATELY, in order truly to enjoy ocean racing, it is helpful to be rich. A middle-class ocean racer costs a quarter of a million, and as has been previously remarked, if you have to ask the price of operating it, you can't afford it. But there are two ways to be rich—one is to have scads of money, and the other is to want less. For sailors who can't handle either option, there is the Other People's Boat Club (the O.P.B.C.). One becomes a member by having skills approaching those of Dennis Conner, learning to keep one's mouth shut under duress (not for you, Ted Turner), and keeping one's name modestly known. You have really become a member when professional skippers on famous ocean racers know you by your first name and owners send you Christmas cards. As yet, the club has no burgee, no clubhouse, no honorable secretary, and no formal procedure for achieving membership. Members of long standing do, however, have a uniform—it consists of a drawerful of LaCoste shirts with various boat names embroidered thereon, together with pocket patches from the Admiral's Cup, the Onion Patch Series, the Southern Cross, the Clipper Cup, the SORC, or the Big Boat Series.

In the honored past, Sherman Hoyt and Ducky Endt were founding members. Ducky, to the end of his life, was a member in good standing, but Sherman, named after his Uncle Cump (General William Tecumseh Sherman) had his distinguished predecessor's irrepressible tongue. He widely admitted that he had saved the America's Cup for Mike Vanderbilt by seducing Tom Sopwith into a calm spot. Having shamelessly usurped the limelight, Hoyt never again crewed with Vanderbilt. One club rule obviously is to be known as helpful rather than vibrant. Being too good isn't as good as being very good.

I've always found being pretty good easier than being superb. I'm medium in size, intensity, skill, and intelligence—a quick study rather than a genius. As a navigator, I've always been able to find my way into the barn, regardless of fog, rain, or the dark of night, and yet I am endlessly baffled by the questions deep and yearning students of navigation think up to ask me. I'm a good enough cook to prefer my own cooking to the average crew member's, a good enough sail trimmer to fill in till sailmakers begin tweaking and barber hauling, a good enough helmsman to surf most waves off the wind and to steer in small increments on the wind. I weigh enough to work the winches, have fast enough hands to stop the spinnaker briskly, and enough wit to enjoy conversation. In heavy weather, my terror level is close enough to the surface to shorten down before the boat leaves the purlieus of control and the off-watch owner storms into the cockpit. And, of course, I love sailing.

Now there are those infected with the sailing virus who are content to manipulate their own small craft in their own small world, relaxed in the cockpit and attentive to the whispering wave, the wandering zephyr, and the delicate relationship between sail, tiller, trim, and balance. Like maiden aunts in perfumed boudoirs who read tales of roaring passions and sink into light and dreamless sleep, they can know about it without wanting to try it. But your regular O.P.B.C. member cannot get his excitement vicariously; he needs a half-million-dollar boat, a sail inventory numbered in the thirties, oceans to cross, and nations to conquer. He needs a job that gives him time off, intermittent income, basic clothes, and good contacts.

I fell into the O.P.B.C. by recognizing both need and chance when they fell into my lap. Skippering a P.T. boat in the South Pacific allowed me to forget much of the laborious learning that had let me teach Chaucer, Milton, and Nineteenth-Century Poetry at Clark University; and my early vacations as an assistant professor let me sail most of every summer. I had also managed to move from owning a twenty-five-foot boat to owning a thirty-two-foot boat. And I'd done a little racing with college friends. I was ripe.

Our war over in 1945, I rethought my priorities. Did I want to turn mushroom gray in libraries, footnoting minor articles about major poets, and ending my life with three references to my work in the *Encyclopedia Britannica?* Did I want to live in a city? I wanted my children to grow up, as I had, ranging the woods, swamp, and waterfront; I wanted to spend my working hours within walking distance of home, wife, family. So I applied to three boarding schools with good harbors and ended up in Newport, Rhode Island, at St. George's.

In the fall of 1949, the art instructor, Bill Drury, invited me to come sailing on the recently launched *Bolero*, seventy-two feet of black, sleek, S&S racing machine. Her owner, John Nicholas Brown, was chairman of our board of trustees and Commodore of the New York Yacht Club.

We had a marvelous afternoon. It was one of those hard, bright fall days, with a dark sky, brilliant light, and the confined waters of Narragansett Bay brisk with a thirty-knot wind and a short chop. *Bolero* muscled to windward under main, staysail, small jib top, and mizzen at nine to ten knots, throwing out great flat sheets of spray and moving with the massive authority of a locomotive. Her professional crew, Captain Fred Lawton, Archie, Kris, and Joe (the cook) were quite busy on each tack, what with runners to let go and take up, and two sets of sheets. I deserted the conversation of my elders in the cockpit for the mid-deck, and was soon grinding away on the coffee-grinders and doubling across the deck to tail the runners.

At one point, Commodore Brown, deep in conversation with Drury and Ken Safe, casually tacked without giving notice. Captain Lawton, Archie, Kris, and I just made it through the tack, Joe being below. Once the tack was completed, and we were snoring along the shore of Prudence Island, Captain Lawton stamped his way grimly from the foredeck aft to the cockpit. There, hands on hips, he glared at the Commodore and spoke thus: "Commodore! Leave us have no bloody secrets from the foredeck!" Brown turned the helm over to Safe, followed Lawton to the foredeck, and patted and soothed him into docility.

Meanwhile, I'd been taking pictures of it all. When we were again moored at Ida Lewis, I stayed on deck and helped put things away while the first round of tea was poured. Then, all being secure, I went below and expressed my enthusiasm—the difference between *Bolero* and my *Wagtail* being like hunting tigers instead of making a daisy chain. Still heightened, I spent the evening in the darkroom, and delivered twenty 8 × 10 prints to Harbor Court in the morning. Two days later, John invited me to be a regular member of the racing crew, an awesome group including Corny Shields, Olin Stephens, Doc Davidson, Dick Goennel, and, later, Arnie Gay and Fred Temple.

Everyone knew more than I did, and on *Bolero*, the penalty for ignorance was doing the hardest job. In every maneuver, the deck crew dashed for the nearest, lightest job, and I ended up at the coffee-

Commodore Brown and Captain Lawton on Bolero.

grinders until the total process became clear to me. By the end of the next summer, in the NYYC Cruise, I was spinning the genoa sheets off the coffee-grinders while some hapless guest was cranking the handles.

On a big boat, it is well to disabuse yourself of small boat habits. Archie once let the spinnaker sheet loose on a downwind start, and I grabbed the rope tail, thinking to flip it on a winch. As it rose in boa constrictor coils behind me, I made a rapid, involuntary trip down the deck toward the turning block, finally diverting to a cockpit winch and burning my hand to the bone as the line ran through while I got on turns. The forces driving that tonnage are immense. The cleat on top of each coffee-grinder is aluminum, and on one occasion when the released wire sheet wasn't lifted high enough, it caught a turn on the cleat and cut off eight inches by one inch of two-inch high aluminum. In her second spring, *Bolero* raced to Bermuda, finished first, and set a course record. Before the race, for four weekends, a full crew left Newport on Friday evening, sailed out to sea, and drove her through heavy seas to see what would break. One night, the snatch block on the quarter went and the wire sheet cut one stainless stanchion clean off and hairpinned the next.

Eventually, alas, Old White Joe, the cook, retired, and John perforce sold *Bolero* and bought a Block Island 40, which he called *Tango*. On *Tango*, Kitty and I went for a weekend cruise with John and Anne, and Anne threw us out of the cabin while she made dinner—more panicked at feeding four than supervising a feast for forty. But by that time I was known to Sven, to Magnus, to Paul, to Bucky, to Grossmiller, and the regular membership of the O.P.B.C. The door was open.

It let me into some strange rooms. At one point Bill Snaith was building one of the ultimate *Figaros*. Unfortunately, her builder was so meticulous that she was not finished in time for the Transatlantic Race. Dick Goennel and I uneasily got in touch with Rod Stephens, who assured us that we'd be on a competitive boat even if we waited till the last minute for Bill. Finally, Bill called to say it was no go—he was going to have a perfect boat, not a hastily finished one. Two uneasy weeks passed. Then the phone rang. "Gruss," said a guttural voice,

Corny Shields, a member of Bolero's *crew.*

"you are vanlink sailink uber den Atlantisch?" Bewildered I replied, "Ya." "Well, get your butt down to New York. Klaus Hegewisch has a potential winner and needs crew." My interlocutor was George Washington Blunt White—one of the more gamesome of all ocean racers, and Commodore of the Cruising Club of America (CCA).

The trip was in German. The boat was a good one, almost a copy of a Rhodes fifty-four-foot yawl, but with the insides done by the designer of Hegewisch's steamships. For that reason, the head had its uptake close to the waterline and worked, under sail, only on the starboard tack. Our first four days were on the port tack. The crew was a wild assortment: a bookseller from Göttingen, a slightly disturbed

Bolero's *navigator, K. S. M. "Doc" Davidson.*

ex-storm trooper from Hamburg, a sailmaker's assistant from Traver-munde, and an ex-submarine skipper from the *Kriegsmarine,* now a weather analyst from Travermunde. Eric, the meteorologist, listened every A.M. to the "kanarienburds" ditting and dashing, and made a weather map for us with colored pencils.

Forewarned, in mid-Atlantic we got the great-grandmother of storms up our rear, went down to a double-reefed main, and ran at ten to twelve knots for Europe. We weren't really frightened until a search light picked us out at midnight, and we saw a giant tanker battering to windward, each wave breaking the length of her deck and erupting over her five-story bridge. Shortly thereafter we were jibed by a break-ing sea, blew out the main along the reef points, and shook loose the refrigerator, which charged across the doghouse cabin and mashed up the dish locker. We went to storm trysail, and reluctantly, after the storm passed, sewed and set the main rather later than we should have. That, plus getting becalmed under Lindesnes, brought us in second to Dick Nye.

One day after the storm, the ex-storm trooper paid hand refused to sleep forward. He said it was (1) too active, and (2) too wet. Hege-wisch pointed out (with relentless Teutonic logic) that the paid hand slept forward in the cabin designated for *the paid hand!* So the paid hand quit, abnegated his salary, and came aft with the gentlemen yachtsmen. At this point, we ran out of food because, while she was being shipped to New York, the paid hand had entertained various girls in the yacht, largely by cooking with them. He judged it the better part of valor to avoid any mention of a hiatus in good German beer, knack-wurst, butter, etc. The emergency stores were broken out: *schwartzbrot und schmaltz* (blackbread of a sour, dense kind, and lard), blutwurst (blood and fat), and lots of spinach. All in all, the cuisine was difficult to lift above disaster.

Klaus bought Dick and me a splendid meal in the hotel at Mars-trand on the morning of our finish. Good food has never tasted better.

The next summer it was borne in upon me by distaff pressure that

Bolero *finishes first; Bermuda Race, 1950 (Bermuda News Bureau).*

Kormoran *had fish in the cockpit after the storm—Sailmaker Rebien holds;*
Goennel steers.

my membership in the O.P.B.C. had absented me from my family for the last three summers—first a little, for the Bermuda Race (our third child was born two days before *Bolero* got back from Bermuda in 1952) and the NYYC Cruise, and then for more than a month while I twice raced or cruised transatlantic. I thereupon vowed to shape up, bought a Volkswagen bus, put a sailing dinghy rack on top and sleeping accommodations inside, and stowed a tent and cots for us in the dinghy. As a family, we would sail in every lake in the United States—all summer. Unfortunately, the day before the Bermuda Race, Rod Stephens called and asked me to give up four or five days to sail to Bermuda on a new fifty-six-foot Abeking-built S&S yawl, *Kay*, with Sven Frissel, Ironmaster for SKF. Sven had no one on the boat who'd ever sailed the race.

I was packing my bag when Herself came in. "I knew it was too good to be true," she remarked, shaking her head at the inevitability of behavior patterns. Nervously explaining that it would only take six days, and that I could meet her in Chicago, at her cousin Richard's, I continued to stuff my sea bag. In the long silence that ensued, I understood that Kitty had been dubious about my abandoning a sea berth for a Volkswagen. When I called her in Chicago from Bermuda, and explained that they needed me to sail the boat back to Sweden, she made it quite clear that I had only three weeks leave, and could fly over the pole to her sister's in Los Angeles. During that time, she actually had an interesting trip, losing two of the children for half a day in Bryce Canyon.

Kay's crew was fascinating. Ernle Bradford was author of *The Great Seige* (of Malta) and a maritime history called *Mediterranean*. As a naval officer, he had knocked King Farouk flat on the floor of his own palace during a dance in which Farouk attempted advances to Ernle's wife. Within the hour, he was out of Egypt, off the R. N. records, and a (living) nonperson. Our navigator, Michael Ritchey, perennial last-to-finish in the smallest boat in the OSTAR, had been brought up in Albania, where his father, retired from the Horse Guards, ran King Zog's army and kept a 007 eye out for Britain on things Albanian. Mike was honorable secretary of the Royal Navigational Society and knew more about navigation than is decent. Albert (no last name) was heavily bearded to conceal a scar an inch wide that

ran under his chin from ear to ear. A Belgian, he had been left for dead
by the Germans, who in haste had missed the vital arteries. Albert
wouldn't let his picture be taken, and handled all financial transactions
for the boat. Since SKF is associated with Bofors and Oerlikon machine
cannon, I rather suspected that Albert's business was with emerging
nations—although he was aboard under patently false pretenses as
cook. The professional, Sven, dismissed all ports with the succinct
remark, "Marstrand bettra," until we landed in Marstrand in a cold
rain, where he pulled the snapper he'd been saving: "Bermuda bettra!"
Sven Frissel was a dignified, strong skipper, and his red-bearded son
Arne was a true Viking, never happier then when the wind was over
forty and the ship roaring through breakup waves.

I got bumped off the transpolar flight, and took thirty-four hours
to get to California in the same nylon shirt. Kitty's enthusiasm at seeing
me came to an abrupt halt about three feet before contact. For the rest
of the summer we sailed and camped—sailed, actually in twenty-six
lakes, missing only the lake under the Tetons where the Park Ranger,
smilingly watching children in vinyl canoes, refused to let me sail my
wooden dinghy. "Listen, mister, I don't care if you've sailed around the
damned Horn, we're not having any sailboats tip over in This Lake!"

Ernle Bradford and "Albert" on Kay.

For twenty-three years, I was grateful to the O.P.B.C.'s skippers, sailing with Curtis Bok, George Moffett, Tom Watson (not the golfer), Hank duPont, Dick Nye, Bill Snaith, two out of the three sailing Triminghams, Gubelmann and Ridder, Bates McKee (whose grandson is an Olympic '84 champion sailor), Rudy Schaeffer, Thor Ramsing, Huey Long, and Sir Max Aitken. Twenty-three years of state-of-the-art boats, of Bermuda, Cowes, La Rochelle, Newport, Marstrand, Oslo, Copenhagen, Travermunde, Capetown, Rio, Santander, Bayonna, Greenland, Hamburg, and St. Malo. In the process, of course, one gets older, but the O.P.B.C. (like the Internal Revenue) even has provisions for aging. One follows The Sequence. In the hot blood and high energy of youth, one inhabits the foredeck. On *Bolero*, before dacron, the sixteen-ounce genoa weighed 400 pounds dry, and never went up or came down dry—a task for heroes. Every sail was stopped and stowed as it came down, and carried forward by three souls in a long snake. Once sails were set, the deck apes then manned the winches, quickly taking in two-ton loads each tack, thus making round-the-buoy racing, the owner's delight, into the crew's testing ground. If you couldn't stand that heat, you were not reinvited to that kitchen. Meanwhile, we honed other skills.

The first step into middle age is getting to be a trimmer. In every race, around the buoys or across an ocean, the sails are trimmed constantly. With winches, minor adjustments aren't enervating, and one hand on the tail and the other on the handle is easy. On tacks, the trimmer is the tailer, keeping tension as the grinders spin the handles to a blur. At times, in middle age, if you make the mistake of getting on the handles, you find you can't keep up with the ox on the other side!

Slowly, slowly, now, you ease toward the cockpit, first as mainsheet trimmer, and then as helmsman. A helmsman's skills are developed in either small boats, your own boat, or on Transatlantic Races, where the trip is too long for two helmsmen to do all the steering. Your O.P.B.C. member can frequently parlay his reputation on major racers into getting the helm from lesser owners. Failing at helmsmanship (and there are those who never get a sense of ship, wind, and sea), navigation is the next step toward senility. The navigator's task has been electronically eased in recent years and has become much more precise, but I can remember a Capetown-Rio race with *Xanadu II* where I took sights very frequently, day and night (full moon, clear air in the South Atlantic), and changed course about every three hours. We did a lot better than was expected.

I can remember a marvelous old buff, a director of the Bank of England, Sandy Sandison, who cooked for us on Dick Nye's *Carina* on a Fastnet. He bought all the food, stirring Dick, who would eat any-

Sandy Sandison on Carina.

thing, anytime, with energetic indifference, to simulated horror at the reckoning. "What does he think this boat is, Twenty-one?" Sandy wrote a book about his ultimate service in the O.P.B.C. called *To Sea in Carpet Slippers* (with illustrations by Hoyt). He cooked, and raced, well past his late retirement.

But, ultimately, one loses a taste for racing. In heavy weather, on our *Telltale II,* I continually repeat the cruiser's two mantras: "Wait a half hour" and "We're cruising!" My gung-ho son, sailing with us to the Virgins with head winds at twenty-five to forty, sneaked out a reef, put up the working jib, and shortly (the wind rising again) had us crashing along, rail under, in the best racing style. I forebore erupting from well-earned unrest until the change of watch, and reporting ten minutes early, let the adventurers change down. "Next time. . . ." I started. "I know," he nodded, "wait . . ."

Eventually, then, taste, muscle tone, and the pauseful finger on life's headlong train attenuate your qualifications for the O.P.B.C. Must you thereupon dessicate, now and then cooking or navigating a desultory short race, or worse, doing something stupid like buying a house on a small lake or river? Never. The time has come to join O.B.S., the Owner's Boating Society. Ancient, bearded solons like Don Street and Ken MacKenzie acquire their own boats, and, sitting lordly at the helm, convey wisdom to grateful charterers. Or selling the family manse and embarking as live-aboards, we happy few retirees invite future generations of O.P.B.C. members and past owners and companions to come cruising, not over thirty miles a day, in good weather, with us. Who knows what pearls we may cast, what gaudy reminiscences we may improve together?

Proposed Burgees

4

This Butter Has Hairs in It

I'VE ALWAYS BEEN very close to my dogs. At the age of ten, I shot the milkman with my bow and arrow because he'd run over my wire-haired fox terrier. After the milkman got out of the hospital, my father threatened to take away my archery equipment if I ever did it again. Penrod, the fox terrier, left such a hole in my heart that my next dog did not come until after my heart was repaired by marriage. Kitty and I devoted a winter's poker earnings—we played Sunday nights with our grad school friends for a nickel limit, and paid off the books before Easter vacation—to buying a pedigreed pup from the George Vaills. They bred liver and white springers out in Woodbridge.

We named her Sherry, which was short for Scheherazade, because she kept us awake nights to suppress her whimpers. We wanted to keep our dog-forbidden apartment until spring vouchsafed my doctorate. The American Kennel Club, a group of arbitrary deciders, turned down three names in a row—Elizabeth Barrett Browning ("no people's names"), Flush ("already taken"), and Scheherazade ("no such name"). Her certificated name became Mistress Browning. She lived for our approval, and was very smart—the smartest animal we'd lived with until we had our first child. She would go into the kitchen and close the door on herself during dinner; she would retrieve a golf ball driven deep into a hayfield; she learned to swim to seaward of our baby, Katy, and herded her beachward whenever Katy's bellybutton approached immersion. The one thing she couldn't learn to do was sail.

We took her cruising with us, but a heeling boat filled her with dire apprehensions. Whenever we thrashed to windward, heeled down and carrying a strenuous helm with a long tiller (*Wagtail* was a a double-ender with an outboard rudder), Sherry had to be in my lap, preferably with her head alongside my neck, where she could hear murmurs of consolation over the wind. While her ears flipped into my mouth and eyes, I had to cross my legs and brace one across the cockpit to keep her from spilling off, despite her frantic clinging by leg and claw. Come tacking time, I had to dislodge her leg by leg, and then accept her on the other side as we came through the wind.

Sherry's presence was wonderful for Kitty because I was so dog-bound that Kitty had to do all the winching in of our double-head rig and runner backstays. The exercise fought Cooper's droop in grand style and gave her a perky chest profile. It was also good for me, as it kept me out of the icebox and diminished snacking. Katy, aged one, was mildly jealous.

Running before the wind, Sherry wandered about, happy as a dog afloat could be. We tried to train her to use a plastic doormat for her kidney and bowel functions, but a springer, once trained to the out-doors, keeps the faith. We even saved some of her stools, rubbed them in the mat, and encouraged her to sniff it. She cowered in embarrassment and self-induced disgrace for hours thereafter, while I washed and cedar-perfumed the mat, blushing at my gaucherie. However stern her sanitary discipline was, her urges were, nevertheless, normal. Dogs, as all dog lovers know, have a briefer urine-cycle than people. The result was that, before the wind, Sherry would point fixedly toward the near-est land and simulate heartbreak, her body elongated, her nose sniffing the remote good earth, and her enunciation thin and piteous. Coupling sympathy with exasperated annoyance is psychically difficult, but I tried.

As a natural corollary of her landwards yearning, particularly after a long and trying day's passage, getting ashore became a categorical imperative. As we backed the anchor in and tested its bite, the dinghy would attack the stern, and Sherry, highly motivated, would leap from deck to dinghy, bark commandingly the second I appeared aft, and then stand up in the bow on full alert as I rowed toward the distant shore. Meanwhile, I yearned for a cool drink in the cockpit, unencumbered by dog. To my credit be it said that I never seriously contemplated giving her away for the three and a half months that constituted the scholastic summer vacation. Who, I ask you, could endure three and a half months with a mourning springer? Kitty suggested it, motivated, I fear, by subliminal jealousy. Kennels were out, for when we returned after having left her for a week in one, she ran toward us yelping, squatting, and peeing in a paroxysm of relief and gratitude at escape from what, to her, might well have been a life sentence.

In our second summer of dog-child cruising, we arrived at a partial solution to Sherry's balance problem. We'd replaced a light pram with a stable, fat, wide-sterned Oldtown dinghy that towed beautifully. We also bought a sort of dog vest, a canvas washable that was a cross between the sling you use to carry logs to the fireplace and a corset. It had holes for the front legs, was soft, and laced on. It provided a handle on her back. In light to medium air, I'd transfer her to the dinghy, where she rode to windward in our flattened wake with obvious pleasure, sniffing the informative air, and letting the wind lift her ears. In heavier seas, we'd luff up, loft her aboard, and go back to routine number one.

But we never solved the endemic problem of the long-haired dog in the summer—shedding. The planking on our cabin sole was painted, as was the oak companionway. The decks were painted canvas, with some tooth. There was nothing to inhabit the redistribution of shed hair except mildly adhesive materials, like towels, washcloths, and alas, butter. Thus, even asleep, Sherry was a universal presence.

The other major problem she offered was embarrassment at the bathing beach. I've said she was very bright, in some ways brighter than people. The problem of staying afloat, for instance, as solved by Sherry, would eliminate drowning, PFDs,* and water wings. In the water, while she swam, she'd swallow large quantities of air, inflating her stomach to equal her chest, and swimming along triumphantly, eyes and mouth above her waterline. Then she'd come ashore. Like every dog, she had a progressive shake that started with her head and moved slowly aft along her body to her flaglike tail, emitting an arc of bright

*Personal Flotation Devices.

Sherry shares a picnic with Kitty, Katy, and Wm. B. on the beach at Tarpaulin Cove.

spray up to four feet from her body. Kitty and I are both swimming nuts, and as we, dog, and children liked beaches, we swam from the shore. By attentive chaperoning, we could control her shaking area, but her subsequent activity was too prolonged and widely audible to be managed. She'd stretch herself comfortably on her belly in the sand, and emit resonant rectal zephyrs until her substitute swim bladder was deflated. Too often, these directed attention and suspicion to us. Of course the farther north we got the fewer people were swimming, and on, say, Roque Island, her peculiarity went unnoticed.

As our cruising pattern developed, in those early years, we'd move lazily east, visiting friends in Pine Orchard, New London, Watch Hill, Martha's Vineyard, Manchester, Marblehead, Cape Ann, Chebeague Island, and Boothbay. Meanwhile, we'd manage to strike up friendships with other cruising couples—one year the Morrisons, another the Isoms—and we'd cruise in loose company. Sherry didn't mind our absence when we visited friends ashore—we would leave her to romp with other dogs, while we went shopping, dining, or partying. Ashore, like us, she loved hikes over the dunes and downs, or through the woods to Jordan Pond, up from the docks to Blue Hill, or just wandering the dusty Maine roads. Frequently, when we went ashore and stopped to converse extensively with chance acquaintances at, say, Buck Harbor Yacht Club, she'd take off by herself in full confidence, her flag wagging, to smell out the surroundings. If she didn't find us later, she'd be waiting, expectantly, in the dinghy. Ashore, she felt confident and independent.

As it turned out, this confidence was not entirely a good thing. Time had passed. I'd been overseas, and the boat had been put up for a couple years during W.W. II. Sherry was getting more relaxed and heavier. I'd say that, by 1947, she was about a thirty-five-pound dog, and no longer willing to leap into the cabin from the top step of the companionway. Whenever we went below, she had to come, and she'd put her forepaws on my shoulders, flop the rest of her into my arms, and accept lowering to the sole. But she still could leap ashore, particularly to a dock. And thereby hangs the crucial episode of our dog-cruising.

You must realize that even as late as post–W.W. II, yacht clubs were cordial to members of other yacht clubs. You'd even see bulletin boards in local clubs filled with invitations to share the facilities of yacht clubs for two hundred miles in either direction. Today, of course, the cruising yacht club member is passed over to the commercial czars of the harbor with the cordiality of a headwaiter ejecting a leper. The club we outraged was the Edgartown Yacht Club. As clubs go, Edgartown is tightly elegant. The New York Yacht Club generally stops there, and I can remember coming in with Commodore Brown's *Bolero,* the air filled with reciprocating cannon salutes and flags dipping and undipping. Sacred protocol. Flying CCA, which, having no clubhouse, isn't even reciprocal, *Wagtail* tied to the Edgartown Yacht Club dock for fuel, water, and a spot of shopping. It was Sunday noon, and the dining hall was full with ritual Sunday diners as we topped the tanks. By this time, we had two children, Katy who was about five years old, and Wm. B. who was twenty months. And Sherry. She sat around the boat for a bit, and then wandered off through Edgartown, looking for a spot of uncontaminated lawn. Wm. B. was very busy, and I kept shunting him away from the beer opener and the binnacle, away from the ignition keys, until finally I gave him a winch handle and let him wind away. Katy was making colorful scrawls and demanding admiration. There were still anchoring holes in the harbor, and I was itching to get underway and fill one.

When Kitty came back, we cast off, motored away, and never thought of Sherry. She apparently had a watch eye on us, however, and as we slid away from the inshore dock, past the dining room, she belted into the dining area, leaping and barking past tables, from window to window as we passed. She made the porch, saw our stern, hurled back through the tables diagonally to the exit door, and made it to the Three Swallows Club, where she repeated her performance through the late drinkers, then on to what is now the Harman's dock. By this time, we'd missed her, and reversed course; so did she! Harman's, the Three Swallows, and the Edgartown Yacht Club had their second frantic dog visitation, and we, knowing we couldn't possibly now go near the Edgartown Yacht Club, pulled up to the town dock and received a hot, damp, terrified dog. She leapt from the dock straight onto my chest, licked my face frantically, and then yipped around three circuits of deck to let off the anxieties. Toward evening, she stopped panting, but she had to be restrained from bunking with me. We anchored in Vineyard Haven.

Plainly, cruising with a dog had extensive drawbacks, and Kitty and I finally made the only decision open to us. We sold the boat. I embarked on a career of ocean racing, largely transatlantic. My mother would often take the kids and dog for a week or so; we had other friends with boats, and Kitty was pleased either to fly over and join me or to sail the crossing as cook and then go home to Sherry and the children. We missed *Wagtail*, but, after all, we would never again have been able to take her to Edgartown.

5

The Teacher Taut

MY INTRODUCTION TO the magic world of ocean racing in powerful sailboats came because I had been a jock—swimming five miles a day for Yale's great coach, Bob Kiphuth, in the fourteenth through seventeenth undefeated years of the Yale swimming team. A national champion in the three-man medley relay, I had been competently assisted by the world's record holders in the 100-yard breast stroke and the 100-yard freestyle. Any jock is in demand in ocean racing, where walking winches double in brass as movable ballast. Minor experience in sail, frequently capsizing my Barnegat Bay sneakbox in the lagoon below the family summer cottage northwest of Westerly, Rhode Island, plus a good ear for lingo and a cousin who subscribed to *Yachting*, let me talk a good game. All in all, an average beginning.

We raced Frank Bissell's *Dorothy Q.*, a highly competitive Alden yawl, maintained in spit and polish "Bissell fashion." We raced with a passion close to destructive, the spinnaker booming us through night-foggy Fisher's Island Sound (soundless, lightless buoys streaking by on either side) or, rail under, skinning the shoal off Sandy Point. Frank, who broke into tears if you crushed a potato chip on his teak deck at anchor, ignored dark rocks that skinned the keel. Dick Nye once said, "The technique for winning is drawing a fine line between winning and sinking." That's how we did it.

Armed with the vast sailing experience of saying "yes" and doing what Frank said, I next started my first year of gainful employment (if $100 a month can be called that) at Milton Academy, where I taught

N. D. Hoyt in 1937, the teacher at Milton Academy.

English to the seventh-graders (The Mice) and coached them in football, a sport I'd never played much. It was a hard winter, and by spring I yearned for white sails, hot sun, and a boat smashing spray horizontal as it thundered to windward. I had publicized my dream widely, modestly admitting to profound nautical experience, and, as usual, opportunity presented itself handsomely.

When Commodore Robert Stone of the New York Yacht Club was eleven his mother felt that he was too old for a baby-sitting establishment like a summer camp and that he needed to do something that was more responsible, independent, and individual. At the time, she wondered how I was planning to sail the summer away and whether I would consider chartering a boat and taking five boys cruising? (Milton was a Very Good School, and anyone who taught there was, *ex post facto*, RESPONSIBLE.) Before I'd found the ideal yacht (a yawl, *Czarina*, the size of *Dorothy Q.*), I had acquired (besides Bobbie Stone) Harry S., Walter P., Gus H., and a fifth lad who tortured me so little in the course of the summer that I can't recall his name. The others were so independent, so individual, and so prone to assume responsibility that I ended the summer fifteen pounds lighter than I'd begun it. By September, they each knew all my weak points.

Like almost anyone who tries to make a profit with a yacht, I was undercapitalized and overextended. The Stones' butler and Mrs. Stone had worked out a food budget that seemed generous, and I was to get double my school salary. On the other hand, the captain of the Stones' 200-and-several-foot steam yacht, *Acadia*, had wisely not been consulted on expenses. And in planning the budget, it was not taken into consideration that the Stones' household consisted of adults and a child, not children and an adult. Children are voracious, better at discarding than conserving, and left to feed themselves, they are willing to fry anything in a pound of butter. These facts I learned in the first week, and forthwith abandoned the notion of sharing the cooking and the putting away. Almost inadvertently, the little men had co-opted me into the cook's slot.

As a teacher, of course, I felt responsible for their nautical education, and the first lesson on a boat is "everything in its place." In the heat of the day, discarded garments, towels, books, pillows, and tableware festooned the decks. The boat, after the fashion of its 1928 design, was primarily intended for day sailing, and had neither pulpits nor lifelines, just a varnished eight-inch covering board outside her cedar decks, with a three-quarter inch foot ledge to brace against. As a hint, I picked up and stowed things ostentatiously, and the hint not taken, I issued a threat that anything not in its place would go overboard. The first thing to go, as an object lesson, was Walter's pants, which unfortunately had a few bitterly lamented dollars in them. Alert for his reciprocal opportunity, Walter untied my silk tank suit from the handrail, and gaily crying "What's this doing here?" (as I had), cast it overboard. It was riotously amusing to the crew. Thereafter we were all less arbitrary.

Education proceeded apace. By the end of the first week, they could throw her into the wind, drop jib and mainsail, flake them down, and have the jib rolled into a neat bundle and bagged by the time the main was stopped and covered. I meanwhile learned that any time anyone discovered a two-pound jar of peanut butter, it and two boxes of crackers would zoom down the red lanes.

The mizzen staysail and the spinnaker came next on the scholastic agenda. They picked up the mizzen staysail quickly, and it would come down on one side and go up on the other automatically. I also soon found that they could scoff two cases of Coke a day. The spinnaker was a little harder—the helmsman would become fascinated by the complex operation, and would wander from course; the halyard was a two-part operation with double blocks, and the spinnaker had to be hoisted in stops. Hoisting took forever, and everyone but Harry S. ran out of gas. Once hoisted, the spinnaker was broken out by being run out to the end of the pole on an endless line through a pole-end block. The spinnaker was vertically cut, long-staple cotton, and fussy to keep full. Surprisingly, once it was up, they soon learned to trim and/or steer cleverly, and they were better in light air than I could believe. Even though I led each of them through stopping it up, all fifty-five feet, no one seemed to achieve my manual dexterity in throwing double half-hitches of rotten cotton around the long snake while maintaining tension with the knees. It was, of course, impossible to jibe either by dipping or by end-for-ending the pole. The sail had to be dropped, stopped, and rehoisted after the jibe. I had them practice, but it never went quickly or smoothly. "Sir, we're not racing!" became a litany.

Meanwhile, since The Mice were well connected, we were entertained royally in Marblehead, Manchester, and Annisquam. I had made them highly recognizable by uniforming them, for shore expeditions, in red Pendleton shirts and white flannels. And their parents may

N.D.H. at the helm, Walter Paine picks up, Bobby Stone shoots film, and Harry Stone navigates.

have sent out form-letter alerts. At any rate, the Boston Brahmin front came to attention with dinner invitations, and as the young rioted decorously with their peers, I was engaged in formal conversation by our various hosts. The food was good, the drinks served from a tray, and the conversation innocuously explored our possible ports with useful hints. The whole effect upon me, a peasant from Yale among

Skipper Hoyt suggests to helmsman Stone (1983's Commodore of the N.Y.Y.C.) that he observe the compass.

the Porcellians, was a mixture of gentle psychiatric guidance with polite wonder that The Future might be in such hands as mine. After each dinner, I found myself sinking into psychically exhausted sleep.

From Annisquam, we made a straight cut for Portland Head, but not until someone's butler had supplied the boat with six pounds of ground sirloin at a price I had never even imagined for hamburger meat, together with such other exotic items as protein bread, avocados, brussels sprouts, plum pudding with hard sauce, and giant olives. And, oh yes, Earl Grey tea, Scotch shortbreads, and baba au rhum. The Mice accepted all these as their due, and consumed them with remarkable dispatch. I suspected collusion. Now, however, I was free of parental assistance until Boothbay, Mt. Desert, and Campobello.

Our crossing from Cape Ann to Portland was, of course, an overnighter. I got the crew to bed betimes, poled out a genoa, slumped in the cockpit with the tiller under my armpit, and sailed through the night, surveying the surrounding blackness every twenty minutes by the egg timer. We arrived at Chebeague Island around 1000, and the troop went ashore in high delight to visit classmates from Milton, Groton, and St. Pauls. We had guests for dinner and a moonlight sail, and it was made clear to me in discussion the next morning that a pattern of sailing all night, visiting for at least half the day, and breakfast at sea was a superb departure from life at home or school. I found myself co-opted into a twenty-four-hour day, and inundated beyond resistance by their appreciation and delight.

It was necessary to sleep, however, and our next crisis came as I slept during the passage under Seguin Island to Five Islands. The wind died as I slumbered, the dinghy was on a long line. The Mice started the engine to avoid visible rocks, and the painter involved itself with the propeller, stopping the idling engine. In a trice, I was overboard in shirt and shorts, knife in my teeth. Hitting the icy water, I took the usual three agonized inward breaths, dove down, and severed the mess. My absence incited the wind, and they sailed into the clear, as I climbed into the dinghy. I rowed; eventually they took pity on me and luffed up. We had seven feet of painter left and made do. "Boy, Sir," they remarked, "did you *ever* wake up and dive overboard! We thought you'd had a bad dream!"

The realization was slowly crystallizing that I was a sucker for their delight, their enthusiasm, their manipulation. Darkly behind the bright pleasure I was taking with them came the suspicion that they subconsciously, like dogs and cats, knew how to control me. There came the day, for example, when, near Friendship Island, very light air and warm surface water (and a good night's sleep, at anchor) tempted me into swimming alongside. We were drifting under the main, with the genoa dropped. I'd been swimming along quite nicely for about a quarter mile ahead of *Czarina* when, to my astonishment, the spinnaker broke out. They headed up a little, to fill it, picked up to four knots, and went by me about ten feet clear as I hoed-gravel in a vain attempt to grab the dinghy. With infinite skill and villainous cunning, they headed up and off, staying a boat length ahead, for the next mile.

I was confident I could catch them since land was slowly getting in the way. As I clawed along in my six-beat crawl (I'd taken second to Jack Medica in the mile at the Nationals a year earlier), I devoutly hoped my sail drill was remembered enough to get the bag down before disaster. It was, and after a little puff that put them 300 yards ahead, I saw it come down. I began, ever so slowly (making, let's say 3 knots to their 2.7) to gain on them. Alas, or hurrah, when I was 25 yards away, I saw the spinnaker rising in stops on the other jibe, and breaking out perfectly. So! They now knew stopping!

A half mile later everything came down in an orderly fashion, and they anchored off the Pride's house on Friendship Island. I arrived, slopped into the dinghy, and eyes afire and smoke exuding from ears and nostrils, climbed aboard. Grinning from ear to ear, Bobbie (twelve), Harry (fourteen), Walter (thirteen), and Gus (twelve) assured me, "We knew you'd make it, Sir!" followed by, "Sir, we were really racing!" "Stopping isn't so hard, once you get the hang of it." "How'd you like those sets?" etc.

I looked dourly at their glow of amusement and success. "You damn near gave me heart failure," I scowled. "If you *ever* . . ."

I'll pass over the festivities on Mt. Desert, where three families were connected. Walter P.'s butler did hideously expensive shopping for me (one does not shop one's self, it seemed), and the P.'s presented me with two cases of Heinekens, thus precipitating a constant battle to keep The Mice, all of whom assured me they were allowed to drink beer at home, from drinking it. I took on a selfish, one-way attitude toward this gormless tale but was subjected to comic throes of death from thirst whenever I clutched a greenie. Two of them by now had learned to pour a Coke directly down their throats, without swallowing, and then fetch a gigantic belch. I began to wonder how well *That* would play to the drawing room.

In fact, my tensions, once I had the group well in hand and checking courses, setting sails, handing, and steering with some skill, began to look down the road to responses from the home fronts. Their language became less restrained, their comic skills exaggerated, their constant "Sir"ing more ironic, and, in general, their behavior pattern, in the Miltonic phrase, "Flown with [the] insolence and wine" of independence. But would Mrs. Stone, and Msses. S., P., and H., like it?

Also, their letters exaggerated their freedom to manage on their own—the swimming chase of the spinnaker, for example, would certainly raise the hair on the owner's neck, pale his insurance agent's brow, and do me little good with headquarters. Subtle censorship suggested itself.

The major psychic shock of the trip was at Campobello, when my gaudy contingent returned to the boat with an invitation to dinner *chez* Roosevelt! They had on their red shirts and white flannels, now less than pristine. I wore gray flannels and a white shirt, pristine. They enchanted Himself. I was included in minor comment and desultory questions. We ate around an outdoor grille—hot dogs in buns, coleslaw, and some delicious ice cream, hand-cranked in relays.

Sailing east of Campobello is fascinating. By going inside or outside of islands, as the tide turns, one can carry the furious currents of the Bay of Fundy to St. John's harbor. In search of a perfect score with current, we valiantly set the spinnaker the next morning and swept all the way to St. John's harbor. The entrance, on a flooding tide, was colorful. The *Lady Hawkins*, bound out, came down the narrow channel, we came up it under spinnaker and with a sturdy following sea swinging us about fifteen degrees off a straight course to either side. The *Lady Hawkins* maintained a whistle obligato to our course changes, obviously expecting us to sheer off at once on one course or another. But my chart showed clam flats on either side of the channel, and gave no indication of how much of the twenty-foot tides covered them. Fathometers were big ship stuff then, and our speed made lead and line senseless. Anyway, one of The Mice could be towed overboard by it.

Directly behind the *Lady Hawkins*, local types were spreading nets across the channel, and gesturing us out of the channel. No way! We sailed over net after net, and were pursued for reparations by the fishermen who now had fishless positions. As we went over the nets, all the corks on either side would pop under, and then bob up behind us since *Czarina* had a straight keel, a wheel aperture, and a rudder shaped like half a valentine heart. Surrounded by screeching fishermen, we made harbor, slanted into a lee, and fed out miles of chain. We had cleared the *Lady Hawkins* by several feet and several shaken fists. As we settled to the anchor, I swallowed my heart and helped stop the spinnaker. The fishermen had mysteriously disappeared, and alongside us were the R.C.M.P., in their harbor launch. "If you want to get up the river," they informed me," you'd better hurry. You won't make it against the tide."

A chain gang got up the anchor, we reset the spinnaker, and took the current around some minor bends. By the pulp mill, the breeze got too complex, so we took down the spinnaker, jibed the main in the fresh breeze several times, and then reset the spinnaker for a run of about five miles to the Royal Kennebecasis Yacht Club. There we were greeted by several club officials, a reporter, and a photographer. We were photographed as the first yacht successfully to carry a spinnaker through the Reversing Falls in years! I regret to state that the Reversing Falls were news to me. I had planned to read *The Pilot* at anchor in St. John's Harbor.

The Mice were delighted, bought papers, and wrote elaborate letters home. I offered to mail them, got a ride into town from the locals, and concealed the evidence. I wondered how chairmen of the board, directors of insurance companies, and anticipators of trends would view a brash youth who played it by ear. What was their Need to Know?

I'll pass over our cruise of Grand Lake, our scraping by two chip barges in the narrows, our long thrash back to Nahant, Massachusetts, in a prevailing southwester alternated with fog and Northeast drizzle. We eased around Nahant neck, anchored in *Czarina*'s home harbor on the last day of August, whence I telephoned the parents. Come the dawn, we had a last meal aboard, The Mice bade me an earnest and loving farewell, and I barely escaped tears of both affection and relief at seeing them safely into the hands of their chauffeurs, each of my multimillion-dollar responsibilities still in one piece. Just wait till the cleaners saw those white flannels!

Thoughtfully, that afternoon, I bought stamps and mailed their newspaper clippings and highly colored accounts of St. John's Harbor. In my 1928 Chevvie convertible, delivered with a season's crocheted fenders by my younger brother, I trundled my dirty summer clothes home and entered Yale Graduate School. I didn't have enough education or maturity to deal with kiddies, so I decided to try college teaching.

I next saw Commodore Robert Stone in 1983, giving the America's Cup away on Mike Vanderbilt's back porch. With sly charm and impeccable prose, he attributed the victory to Ben Lexcen, deliberately ignored Alan Bond and Warren Jones, architects of the NYYC's summerlong embarrassment, and turning his back on the eager Bond and crew, gracefully presented the cup to the Commodore of the Royal Perth Yacht Club. I proudly recognized the delicate torture; its birth pangs were my own!

6

A Night to Disremember

THE SUMMER I TOOK the high-gloss Bostonian young cruising, I existed in a black, unreconstructed state of "getting-on-with-it," brought about by my impressionable youth and the fact that I'd never cruised at all—just ocean raced with Frank Bissell, who drove *Dorothy Q.* with a fine frenzy. Getting the most out of sail and ship was a religion, more speed was a mania. On top of that, time was running thin, since I'd promised the 'rents that I'd return their heirs by August 30th, when the statute of limitations ran out for children in camps, and since two weeks of regrouping were sartorially imperative before St. Grotlesex and Exover. So yet again, as night came down on shrinking day, the young were disposed below, unconscious of their peril.

> Irks care the cropful bird;
> Frets doubt the mawcrammed beast.

We'd bade a cheerful farewell to the hospitable Ballards of Chebeague Island, motored around Little Chebeague, and dined under power somewhere off Halfway Rock. When the evening breeze filled in off the land, we hoisted sail, main and mizzen first, and then sheeted out the light genoa to the end of the main boom. The stem chewed up a gentle snarl of water, the steam gauge gave us four knots, and we were off on the long, open-water run from Cape Elizabeth to Annisquam. One by one, the young faded down from chatter to even breathing, and I was alone at the tiller, stoutly bundled against the night's cold.

It was lovely at sea—stars, crisp air, and the moon peering palely over the stern. The after end of the cockpit sloped up from sole to deck at just the right angle for comfort, and with a cockpit cushion under my butt and back, the tiller under my armpit, and the brass teepee of the binnacle glittering in the moonlight and glowing compass-red, I could watch the sails, steer, doze, and ignore whatever might be approaching the tender wood of the hull from dead ahead. At four knots I could not worry. Two hours drifted by; I began to pick up the moan of the Cape Porpoise whistle.

Unfortunately, by this time, my dinner had digested, and I began to be wakeful. Annisquam was how many miles away? We'd make the Annisquam bar at dead low (averaging four knots). The wind was swinging aft, and it smelled like a dry northeaster setting in. It was not to be wasted. The genoa collapsed behind the mainsail; the steam gauge flagged to 3.5. Time to "get-on-with-it."

I dropped and furled the mizzen, dashing now and then to the tiller to readjust its tie lines in the hope of holding course. The spinnaker pole was a clumsy wooden thing with a leathered jaw, three eyebolts in the outer end, and a clothesline pulley along its length. I lugged it to the mast, rigged its foreguy, afterguy, and lift. Then I hauled the spinnaker pole out to starboard. Main to port, I fed the starboard genoa sheet through the clothesline thimble, and hauled the sail across. The genoa reluctantly filled. We climbed back to four knots. Back in the cockpit, I stuffed the tiller under my arm, managed to lean just right, and we whispered along on course 258. But sleep again defeated me. At five knots we'd have time to shop in Annisquam before we ran the canal to Gloucester. We'd avoid hospitality; the kids could prowl Gloucester while I slept. I could save a day.

Czarina had an enormous passage spinnaker, made of Egyptian cotton, with vertical cloths. It stretched from the end of the main boom to the end of the spinnaker pole, flattened, to be sure, across the headstay, but adding about 30 percent to the total area of mainsail and genoa together. It was stopped into a giant snake; since there were no winches, it went up on a multi-part halyard.

I was now wide awake and filled with zeal. I dragged the spinnaker from the cockpit locker, took off its bottom stops, frog-legged it with rotten cotton, and dragged it forward. I dropped the main into its lazy jacks, clotheslined the genoa inboard and dropped it. I hauled the frogs-legs outboard, passing around the headstay, and attached the halyard. I dashed aft to check the course, which was AOK. The wind seemed a little better now, possibly because we were down to two knots and fading. In a faint way, I hoped that some of the activity would have disturbed at least one of the sleepers, but they slept resolutely on. I checked the course again, admired the moon and stars, contemplated the cold ocean, placidly bearing the Labrador Current southwest, and disregarding a cautionary impulse, went forward and laid hands on the spinnaker halyard.

Up she went! I hand-over-handed, dropping my butt into the action, my back to the bow, the halyard line piling up at my feet under the mast cleat. Behind my back, I heard an ominous popping sound, looked around, still hoisting, and the damned spinnaker was breaking out up from the frog-legs. In seconds it would be overboard, wet, under the keel, ruined, and a disaster. I hoisted with resolute dedication, unconsciously backing up as one does to get a kite into the air, and backed straight overboard! *Czarina,* day sailor that she really was, had no pulpit, no lifelines, and only a three-quarter inch toe-rail.

The Gulf of Maine was cruelly cold. I took three quick breaths, all inward, as my heavy clothing let the water in against my warm skin. Then I was dragged aft of the boat—heavy, heavy. In the middle of all this, I got both hands onto the halyard, and wrapped it around my wrist.

Meanwhile, my aft progress was hoisting the spinnaker, and as it broke out, filled, and pulled, *Czarina* accelerated. Facedown in the water, I acquired a bow wave as the halyard two-blocked, rolled my head to the side as in crawl-breathing, and grabbed my fourth breath. The acceleration continued, and I had to roll over on my back to get the next breath. My heavy sweater seemed to be streaming back to my knees, the wrap of line cut into my wrist, and I wondered how long I could hang on. If I let go, would anyone wake up? Could I get rid of my waterlogged clothes and swim as far as the boat? Would the mess

of coils jam and the boat sail on forever? My frantic thoughts were
ended by a heavy blow on the head.

The spinnaker, it happened, was pulling harder than I was, and the
three-part halyard had pulled me against the towed dinghy. Gratitude
flooded my mind, and keeping my wrist-wrap for assistance, I grabbed
the dinghy's transom, pulled myself past the dinghy to the boat's
transom, and was half lifted aboard by my anguished wrist. The cockpit
had a quarter-bit, to which I made fast the halyard. I walked the rest
of the line forward, took a turn on the mast cleat, and two-blocked the
spinnaker again. Its skirt dripped slightly. I made my wet way aft to
the cockpit with a generally relaxed feeling that it had been a close one,
but we'd made it, and that was that. I removed the dry seat cushion,
settled down out of the wind beside the tiller, got her on course, and
noticed with satisfaction that the steam gauge registered over five.
Mission accomplished! I'd relax till I got my breath and drained a little,
and then get dry clothes on.

But as I slumped beside the tiller, total terror flooded me, colder
than the Labrador Current. I broke into icy sweat; tears streamed from
my eyes; I went limp as wet toilet paper; I shook and my teeth chat-
tered. A night to disremember!

The young slept resolutely on; I never told them how my clothes
got wet, thus preserving my flawless image. Well astern, I could hear
the Cape Porpoise whistle moaning over the cold Atlantic.

7

Weekends with Rosie

WHEN KITTY AND I were still pinned to coastwise cruising by our small sloop, we were, year after year, the enthusiastic guests of Rosie, the Irish Hurricane. We loved her, and she, God bless her, loved the whole world. Infinitely ready and eager for whatever came next, she was Lady Bountiful to all her family and any reasonably competent friends who would sail with her. And she sailed for at least eight months a year. After a succession of Concordia Yawls, she commissioned K. Aage Nielson to design her a gaff-rigged schooner, probably at the instigation of Pete Culler, one of her various professional captains.

Culler was famous within his particular cult. Half naval-architectural historian, half ritualized wooden boatbuilder, and wholly opinionated, he played the rich role of Captain Culler to the hilt, disapproving of dacron, fiberglass, aluminum, sail tracks, winches, cruising as opposed to cargo-carrying, and instrumentation subsequent to the lead-and-line. Any boat with a "Bermuda rig," he felt, belonged in Bermuda. And any craft whose sheerline didn't swoop from a skyward bowsprit to the water and back up to a balustrade around the back porch excited his scorn. All the tools in his shop were hand tools, and every hand tool had its silhouette painted on the wall, around the brackets that supported it. He had a passion for brackets, and could spawn a pair overnight, given the ghost of an opportunity. He was a good skipper and a good helmsman, and he never designed or built

---

Miss Rose B. Dolan, clear-eyed and steady on the helm.

anything that wasn't capable of icebreaking.

Once Rosie's schooner was completed, deadeyes, lanyards, cat-headed fluke anchors, belaying pins, mast hoops, and all, including vertically cut canvas (for heaven's sake) sails, Captain Culler was in his element. He eagle-eyed her around New England. And, Bristol fashion, he maintained her dark green hull, her pale gray cabin trunk, her infinitely molded white trim, her turned balustrade, and her oiled fir deck and slushed masts.

Of course it was Rosie's boat, and since the truth must be confessed, she was a competent helmsman under sail and at sea, but a menace at close quarters under power. With the calm and confident coaching of one of her other captains, Tom Waddington (who never showed the least sign of pressure), she could maneuver adequately and back into a dock without substantially altering the set of the pilings. Culler's premature, detailed, and extensive instructions got her up-tighter than an "E" string, and didn't do his dire apprehensions much good, either. With Captain Culler, she gave up docking—it was worth it for the pride she could take in the perfectly maintained and styled *Defiance*.

Culler's worst fault was his passion for exhibiting tools. He loved them. They were functional instruments, leaving no doubt of their purpose, magnificently more reasonable than people. *Defiance* was a centerboard schooner, and as such, had a centerboard winch ("Oogie" Nielson liked them) and a winch handle. A winch handle is a tool—direct, functional, a plain statement of purpose, a positive silhouette. It lived on a shelf just inside the companionway, about four steps from the winch on the after end of the cabin trunk. The after end of the cabin trunk was the only place on the spreading deck around the cockpit where one could sit, legs extended, back supported, and watch the world and the helmsman. It was thus perennially occupied by one of us.

It came as no surprise that this enticing area of blank support appealed to Captain Culler's decorative instincts, or that, when we arrived to sail one weekend, it sported two brackets and the winch handle, socket up, grip down. Our only surprise was that Culler hadn't painted its profile behind it. Now the whole cockpit lacked any spot with back support. *Defiance,* without finicking yachting comforts, seated the helmsman on the sloping, hard-edged wheelbox, the crew on the broad, dark decks. She was as severely functional as a Gloucester fisherman.

In addition to being a yachting town, Newport is noted for the fine arts, and with one horrified look at Captain Culler's achievement, we scampered ashore to Wiseman's Art Store and made a vital purchase. Come the next morning, those who visited the cockpit found, under bracket and handle, beautifully lettered in Times Roman one-inch capitals (with rub-on letters) "CAPTAIN CULLER'S REVENGE." Two weeks later there was no sign of either bracket or handle in the cockpit, and no change of expression on Captain Culler's face.

Time was passing, and the next year Culler was too occupied with building the character schooner *Integrity* to enjoy cruising as Rosie's coach. She hired Bruce Burgess, then a junior at Yale, to live aboard *Defiance* and keep her up to snuff. Bruce was a free spirit of the finest type, quick, humorous, capable, somewhat imbued with the wooden-boat, deadeyes and lanyards mystique, and given to opinions as strong at Rosie's own. Rosie and he had occasional amicable disagreements (known as "French discussions") in which they pounded the table and yelled at each other. Both enjoyed them, even when they caused uninformed guests to cower.

Bruce had a keen sense of adventure, and Rosie was always ready for something new, so he suggested that she sail *Defiance* across the Atlantic and cruise the Norwegian fjords. The Atlantic was not part of Rosie's picture, but she agreed to meet us in Norway and left us to round up a crew and go. Dr. Richard Warren and I constituted the senior crew; Bruce and a medical school friend, Kari Vetekeinen, and Bruce Lancaster and Dick Ely, two of my best schoolboy sailors, made up the rest. Kitty shipped as cook and den mother.

We had a superb trip across, making two days of over 200 miles, in a (for heaven's sake) gaff-rigged schooner. We arrived in Norway in twenty-one days from Newport. Our arrival was typical of Rosie's close association with the leprechaun and other mystic manifestations. In

Defiance *in the Geirangerfjord; Kitty amidships.*

"*Making over 200 miles for two days in (for heaven's sake) a gaff-rigged schooner.*"

Rosie, Kitty, N.D.H., and five Leicas in the Hardangerfjord.

Bruce oystering in Vikingsvag.

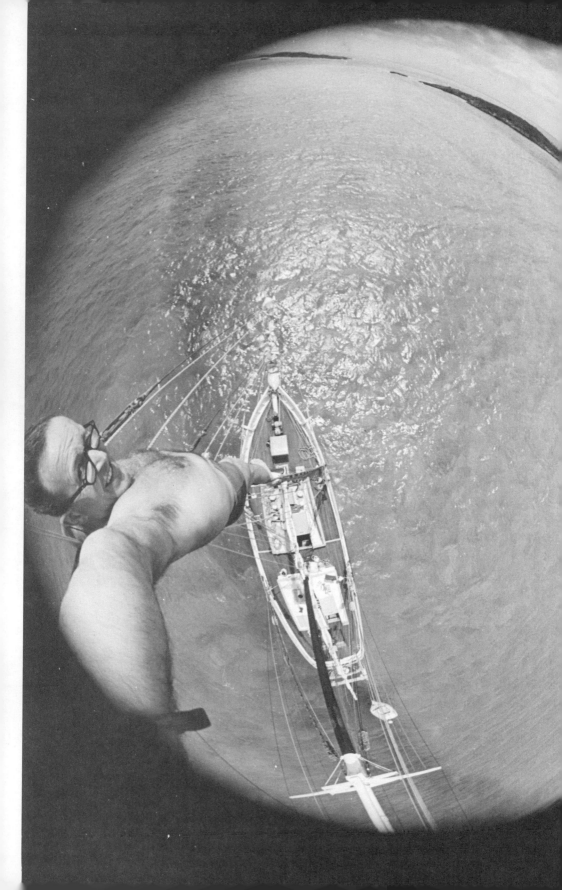

Paris, she had looked into her crystal ball, decided we ought to be arriving in Bergen, and arrived there by plane and taxi exactly one hour before we arrived. The surprise was totally ours.

Rosie was a remarkable, indeed a legendary person. The outfall of a city gas fortune from Philadelphia, she had become a nurse and never married. In World War I she worked as an ambulance driver-nurse-mechanic, and at the end of the war, bought a chateau, hired a faculty, and educated and brought up sixty French war orphans. She joined with Anne Morgan and worked between wars with Friends of France, was given the Legion d'Honneur and other awards by various governments, and worked with the French Underground in World War II. Captured and interned by the Germans, she regularly told all and sundry exactly what they should be doing and how to do it, to the daily terror of those, interned with her, who lacked her certitude. At the war's end, she liberated Baden-Baden, making sure that local institutions got as much of the contraband as possible, "because we Americans always have more than we need." At the age of eighty-seven, she died of spinal meningitis, caught in a small hospital where she went with a chest cold. I'm sure she died totally without fear and completely surprised. It had never been a fate she'd expected. "What's next!?" was her focus.

After we got *Telltale,* she frequently joined us aboard, particularly for going down the Intracoastal Waterway, where every dockmaster greeted her with pleasure. She loved slowly leaving the bright leaves of autumn for the South—the Florida greens, pelicans, palms, and egrets. She took her helm hour with joy, pleaded under power for "a little more juice," hated restaurants, and insisted on washing our dishes. My transatlantic training shuddered at her prodigal use of boiling water, scalding everything at least twice, and squandering gallons per meal. But, like everything else she did, she loved it. I also doubt that she thought anyone else could get them really truly clean.

I think the weekend with Rosie I best remember took place when

---

Defiance and N.D.H. in the Bahamas.

we were still primarily in her debt for such great bounties as an Easter vacation in the Bahamas, a transatlantic cruise, and an exploration of the Norwegian fjords. On this particular weekend, Bruce (then a schoolmaster) was acting as her summer skipper; also aboard were his wife, his small child, Kitty, Rosie, and me. We sailed from Newport to Cuttyhunk, anchored, walked briskly to the top of the island and then down. (Rosie was a redoubtable walker, weighing perhaps ninety pounds and being impatient.) Aboard and still panting, I mixed the drinks, and the girls cooked dinner. The next day we were to rise at dawn (she hated to waste daylight) and leave for Menemsha Bight. The harbor there is tiny, and *Defiance,* about fifty feet on deck, was broad, with an overhanging main boom and bowsprit, and maneuvered with great deliberation. My druthers didn't extend to Menemsha.

We made the entrance by 1000, and my worst anticipations were realized. Some local Massachusetts yacht club or other filled the harbor, rafted in clots in every available space. Fishermen, disbursing fish and local color to the "summa vistahs," occupied every dock. There was no room for us, and I envisaged a pleasant run to Tarpaulin Cove, Oak Bluffs, or Edgartown, all bigger. With our board up, we could even have eased into Tashmoo.

I suggested it, and Rosie's face lit up with a thousand candlepower of delight. "Wonderful," she said, "I have a great idea! I've never been into Menemsha Pond, and the tide's rising, it's almost full. We can make it!"

Perhaps Peter Culler could have made it, but I had prodigious doubts that *Defiance,* with Rosie at the helm, could execute two doglegs in a channel little wider than she was, and with three or four knots of tide across our course. But Rosie's enthusiasm, full of charm and bubble, overbore doubts, and we pressed on toward fate. I stood beside her at the helm, and in measured, calm tones, rehearsed her in the technique of getting the bow swinging before we hit the passage, and then reversing the helm to swing the stern clear as the bow was tideborne into the second alley of the dogleg. The passage is really a witch, sort of like an open "Z" between two sandbanks after a rock ledge.

We left the harbor, went beside the rock wall along the passage to the pond, and were waved at by various local types indolently fishing the tide flow and waiting for an entertaining disaster in the passage. An inhabitant gets several chances a week to watch yachts maneuvering off a sandbar.

Rosie approached the passage with perfect confidence, aplomb, and rather too indolent reflexes. We made it past the ledge, turned slowly, and came with magnificent deliberation onto the sandbank, downtide of the middle leg. We stopped, heeled about fifteen degrees. All the fishermen stood up to watch. Bruce and I went into the routine, and dropped the beautiful lapstrake, heavy dinghy that Pete Culler had built for Rosie. We installed oars and outboard motor, and handed around to the bow, where we dropped an anchor into the dinghy and poured in chain. With the outboard at pitch, we got the first anchor out ahead and on the deep side of the outer sandbar. Then we went back, got another anchor, and took it uptide of the stern, and slightly forward. Back aboard, we led both anchors to the anchor windlass, got Rosie to give the big three-bladed propeller maximum rpm's, and ground away. The tide had risen perhaps three inches, and we pushed forward about three feet before a pile of sand built under the bow by the current sweeping, like a flood, sideways past both bow and stern. Back into the dinghy, and Bruce and I dug sandpile into current until a hollow existed under the stem. Then back aboard, we revved her up ("A little more juice"), and cranked in a few more feet of chain. Another four feet.

Sweating freely, an hour later, and practically at the final peak of the tide, we broke free into the channel, hanging on the anchor over the stern, and engaged in retrieving the bow anchor with the dinghy. We catted it, buoyed the stern anchor chain, baled some 200 feet of it overboard, and finally flung the last of it free and proceeded triumphantly into the pond, where we anchored with the remaining hook.

Rosie was all for rewarding us with the Philadelphia *omnium nostrum*, a stiff shot of old go-fast. We had more serious concerns. The ancient New England custom of wrecking still obtains in the purlieus. We'd left a few hundred bucks worth of anchor and chain in plain view of several deeply interested local spectators, two miles away. The tide was still whooping into the pond, a large area fed by a narrow channel.

The outboard, aided by my full effort at the oars, got us back to the anchor as two other rowboats were tugging it loose from the sandbar into which we had deeply embedded it. Bruce and I thanked them for their efforts, helped them load it into the dinghy, crossed their palms with green gratitude and the gracious assumption that the chain would not have mysteriously been washed out to sea.

By this time the pond was emptying, and the long pull back found us, three and half hours after we'd grounded, making the last hundred yards to *Defiance*.

Rosie embraced us both as we climbed wearily aboard. "Boys! boys!" she enthused, "now wasn't that an adventure! You were wonderful! Everything worked out so well!"

She'd loved every minute of it. Nothing better than taking the slack out of a normal day. We left the next morning just before slack-high, Bruce stemmed a gentle current through the "Z," and as a special reward, Rosie bought us dinner at the Edgartown Yacht Club, with no need to drown the dishes in scalding water.

Our last weekend on *Defiance* came at the end of the summer and was pleasant, but not in the great tradition of the Irish Hurricane. She'd been told by Bruce that he couldn't work summers anymore— his career beckoned. Tom Waddington and Pete Culler, both younger than she was, had had heart attacks, and Pete hadn't survived. Rosie felt that fifty heavy, nosy feet was perhaps too much for her to handle without permanent manpower, and she had put the boat on the market. Our home across the Atlantic, our island in the Bahamas, our excitement in Menemsha, it sold immediately to the Huidekoopers, at Padanarum, and our weekend was to be Rosie's last on *Defiance*. The cruise, again with Bruce, his wife Freddie, young Josh, Kitty, and me, was great sailing. It included occasional French discussions, good food and drink, and a warm nostalgia for the great days of the past. Back in Padanarum, however, the whole affair degenerated into a wake, and Rosie wandered around her lovely boat, wiping down the paint with clean cloths and hot water, stuffing boxes with personal possessions, and generally preparing the body for burial.

I mourn badly, preferring to take my sense of the end of things somewhere else, or seek a viable substitute. So Kitty and I thanked

Rosie, wished her luck with the closing, and drove away. The Huide-koopers and Waldo Howland, gray eminence of the Concordia Yard, were coming out on the dock as we left. We drove home with a feeling of loss depleting our energies, and once back at school, slowly unloaded the car. On the third trip from the garage upstairs, the telephone was ringing, and I answered it.

"Norry!," it said, "is that you?" It was, and the voice on the phone went on, bird cheerful, full of excitement and delight, "It's Rose; you'll never guess what I've done! Waldo showed me the nicest Concordia 41 right here on the dock, and I've bought it." She sounded like Christmas and the birth of the first child rolled into one. My heart leapt up with her. "Now we've got to have radar and I'm going to have good refrigeration," she went on, all plans, ready still for a lot more bright tomorrows.

Last cruise on Defiance—*Kitty with Josh Burgess, W. Burgess, Sr., and Rosie, downcast.*

8

Ham on a Salty Ride

THE MOST INTENSE PERSON I've ever sailed with is Sumner Adams Long, a Boston boy who loves ocean racing as much as he hates to lose. A shipping owner, father of an America's Cup contestant, "Huey," as he is understandably nicknamed, lives in the attic of his emotions. Somehow he can make a melodrama out of almost anything he does. We lesser mortals, his loyal crew, can share his elations, but find it rather more difficult to plunge into his depths of dramatic despair. As actors, we read the parts rather than live them; Huey is a method actor.

The 1963 Transatlantic Race, from Newport, Rhode Island, to England's Eddystone Light, had a script that might have been specifically written for Huey's extravagant talents. As the curtain rose on Act One, Huey and his aluminum yawl, *Ondine,* were drifting through a windless gloom off Brenton Reef, trapped in a fog of frustration. We had shortened the rig for heavy winds and better rating. But in light air, everyone was disappearing ahead of us. Act Two produced two violent storms, and to keep the tension high, a near disaster. But the final curtain found *Ondine* across the finish line, a triumphant overall victor. It was a plot corny enough to satisfy even the histrionic range of the principal actor.

Huey, a kind of one-man Shakespearean repertory, was a victim of fate right at the start. Three bigger boats—Sally Ames Langmuir's *Bolero,* the Italian *Corsaro II,* and Clayton Ewing's *Dyna*—had the mother wit or good fortune to head north of the rhumb line and find wind. *Ondine* and the remainder of the fleet of fourteen yachts sagged slowly through haze and head winds for five days, falling hopelessly behind as the leaders opened a gap of sixty to seventy miles.

Huey agonized, stalked the deck, shoulders bearing the burden of the world. "There goes the ball game," he intoned. "We'll never lick the handicap. We're giving time to everyone down here." But after five days the breeze rose, and with it, Huey's spirits. His Hamlet mood shifted to Macbeth's wild defiance. "The wind's abeam, set the spinnaker!," he ordered. It didn't seem possible to any of us that the boat could carry a spinnaker abeam in better than thirty knots of wind, but the "Lay on MacDuff, and damned be he who first cries hold . . ." mood was on Huey, and we laid on.

Sumner (Huey) Adams Long anticipating the worst.

Ondine's rig, shortened by seven feet, drove her in great style, and we fell off northward before the breeze. Up there, the leaders already had had too much. Our wind increased to half a gale. The seas built. Huey, a skipper perpetually charged with frenzied energy or deep despair for every minute of every race he sails, defied the wind. With

Jim Ivins at the helm goes into a broach.

Still carrying the spinnaker, we go into a knockdown.

The storm fading, young Wm. Hoyt and Chuck Gardella joke; Alex Salm steers.

the velocity at forty knots and gusting higher, he reduced sail (when at all) late, late, late. *Ondine,* a light-hulled craft, cascaded off the top of seas in long, roaring, surfing runs, hundreds of yards at a time. When variations in the wave shapes shouldered her out of her surfing line, the curve of one side of the bow would take over, she'd veer up, broach, jam her main boom deep in the roaring seas, stagger over onto her side (dumping people out of bunks below), and reel back to an explosive refilling of main and spinnaker. Huey put two men on the helm for more power. We carried on. The big 1.5-ounce spinnaker, on a fourth explosive fill, blew out in one great rip, and we wrestled it down. The foredeck was windy and wet, the twenty-eight-foot spinnaker pole thrashed around until we set the number four, a smaller 1.5. It lasted ten minutes.

"Set the storm spinnaker! I am the captain! Set it Now!," Huey roared, arbitrary as Petruchio. We set the bulletproof, a six-ounce nylon, triple-stitched.

Huey collapsed in drugged
sleep; Salm amused at the
helm.

Huey in his race-completed
costume.

With that change of scene, we had the most dramatic moment of the trip. In the dark of 0200 in the morning, a breaking sea under *Ondine*'s stern slewed her while she was surfing at eighteen knots. As though a giant had picked her up, she swung in an instantaneous broach, rudder out of water, nose down, stopped in that attitude, and then, a cross sea breaking behind the first, swung 160 degrees in the other direction, in a full jibe. The boom slammed inboard, fell against the backstay, and cocked up at a 70-degree angle, reefed mainsail flapping wildly. Those in the watch below, staggering to get on deck, were thrown back and forth across the cabin. Bob Davis, the cook, had just extracted six cans from the locker, and as the boat seesawed wildly from beam end to beam end, he was attacked from every side by flying cans.

With Falstaff's discretion, Huey now got the "bulletproof" spinnaker down, started in every seam on at least one line of its triple stitching. We winged out a genoa on the pole. But discretion faded fast. By dawn, he was Henry V, "Into the breach yet once more, oh my comrades!" was the order of the day. "Get it back up, this is still a race!" We rolled the main down to the numbers to keep the head of the reset spinnaker full, and roared on through the breaking, rain-swept Atlantic. Huey's hunger for speed and more speed paid off that day—248 miles for an average of 10.33 knots from a fifty-six-foot hull with long ends. She had closed the gap on all the other boats.

By now, Huey was implacable, and as the seas stacked higher, under the sunlit thrust of a full westerly gale, he could barely be restrained from trying the last 1.5. We managed to satisfy him with a mizzen staysail.

For three days, during which each run was over 220 miles, we gained on every boat in the fleet. One thousand miles from the finish, Ewing's *Dyna*, taking a spinnaker knockdown, had lost her rudder. She managed to finish the race, in the finest tradition, by steering with her sails, but competitively, she was out of it. *Bolero* broke both spinnaker poles, her permanent backstay was carried away, and her mainsail was blown out. Sally Langmuir declared her foredeck a disaster area. The yawl *Windrose*, behind us, reported her position on 13 July as "the sloop *Windrose*," her mizzen and mizzen staysail having gone by the board.

But now the plot changed again. The storm that had driven *Ondine* back into the running had drifted off over Scotland, and the winds went light. Huey's heart went heavy, but the taste of the end was upon him, and he became the magician Prospero, denying the BBC weather broadcast and invoking a new storm. Miraculously, he was right, a secondary low developed a new gale around us as we closed the Channel. The breeze came on, and *Ondine* began again her great surfing runs, this time dead before the wind and dead on course. Huey refused to shorten sail.

The next twenty-four hours were decisive. On a misty night, pitch black and windy, the sea glowed white with spray and phosphorescence. We held onto the big 1.5 spinnaker for three hours, and only went to a reef and the bulletproof when a roundhouse broach brought all hands on deck. We carried on for the rest of the night. For nine hours we averaged 12.2 knots, an unheard-of sustained speed for a vessel of *Ondine*'s size.

Before our anticlimactic finish, without spectators or applause, at 2000 off Eddystone Light, Huey collapsed in drugged sleep, like Juliet, all passion (and energy) spent. We came over the line winners by many hours on corrected time. Landing in Cowes the next day, Huey dressed for still another part—the actor finished with the stage, ready for the street. Painstakingly shaved, with a beautifully tailored suit, NYYC necktie, polished black shoes, and the glossy look of one who's just left the barber, the manicurist, and his valet, he listened to everybody, bought drinks around, and said nothing of the rigors of the voyage. He was the glass of fashion and the mold of form until we brought in the RORC handicap ratings for the Fastnet, two weeks away. Instantly the weight of the world descended. The black despair was upon him. "We are but flies to the Gods, they kill us for their sport!" He was Lear. "We haven't a chance with this rating! How can we compete?" And actually, for the moment anyway, he suffered in the black depths of his drama.

9

Man Overboard

THE FORCES on a large, ocean-going yacht can be lethal. Their potential is amplified by the basic rule of racing—that weight costs speed, and that, therefore, design limits get lighter until something breaks, and then you've gone too far. The total mathematics are further complicated by better materials that set up better strains. After W.W. II, *Bolero* was the latest word in maximum CCA ocean racers. She was seventy-three feet long, weighed twenty-six tons, and had an aluminum mainmast you could not get your arms around. When she was launched, state-of-the-art sails were canvas, and her mainsail, of sixteen-ounce cloth and hand-stitched, needed brutal fists to pound its first slab into a compact roll for reefing. Worse than the main, her number five genoa, the "bulletproof," a bit short on the hoist and barely overlapping the mast, was also sixteen ounces with a three-foot deep reinforcing band along the bottom. It took three men to carry it to the foredeck, dry; it never got forward dry, because it never went up till the apparent wind was over thirty.

Bolero was launched in 1949, and we spent the fall of that year finding out what might go wrong. With a crew consisting of Commodore J. N. Brown, professionals Captain Fred Lawton and cook Joe Gorman, hands Archie and Kris, and an afterguard of Olin Stephens, Corny Shields, and Ken Davidson, plus five vigorous supernumeraries, like me, we went out for three weekends, looking for a storm. The third try, we found it. As it came on, we worked down, sail by sail, from the 1,500-square-foot number one genoa to the 500-square-foot number five. Picture the windy, icy darkness of the North Atlantic to yourself, the waves building with the wind as *Bolero* smashes through seas, now and then scooping 500 or 600 pounds of broken water over her thrusting bow. With the wind screaming, the off-duty watch is roused out, the staysail (300 square feet) hoisted inside the genoa, and the genoa pulled down and pulled aft along the high side. The next smaller genoa is lugged forward, stopped into a long tube by strands of triple cotton string at 3-foot intervals, and hoisted 90 feet up the headstay. Once hoisted, two winch-grinders and a tailer break it out and trim its mad flapping to quiescence. *Bolero*, repowered, accelerates into the sea, smashing and slowing, leaping, dropping, and accelerating. With the spray flying over the windward rail, and seas scooping along the lee deck, the crew next gathers the down jib along the high deck, rolls it into compactness, and ties it with stopping cotton before coiling it aft into its locker.

The wind continues to rise, and four times we reduce acreage. With each change, we make greater speed into the building seas, and the rising wind. Finally under the number five, known in our heroic-joking moods as "the Double-Hernia Jib," we're making ten knots into each sea, bucking through it down to seven, and leaping again to ten. The rain and the spray have saturated the towels round our necks under our rain gear, and water is seeping insidiously down breastbone and belly into crotch and seat. Not for nothing is an ocean passage known in German as a "Seewetfahrt." We supernumeraries on the rail forward of the winches hope the brain trust back in the cockpit ("Brown's Beach") are making us suffer for a purpose.

In the middle of numb misery there's a gigantic "Bang!" The turning block on the after rail, which leads the sheet from the genoa aft and lets it lead forward again to the midship winch, has exploded. Over the wind's noise and the sea's rush, we briefly hear the sheave whupping off into the sky. The wire sheet, which had been getting a jump load of about five tons, has cut one of the three-quarter-inch solid monel stanchions in half and hairpinned the next one. Freed, the number five flaps madly, shuddering all twenty-six tons of *Bolero* as it shakes forestay and mast. Almost as the accident happens, we're forward on the plunging, pitching deck, getting it down, hauling it aft, tying it to the rail. Captain Lawton sets the staysail, and we jog at six knots, running off, while we have a cockpit conference. Olin sums up the consensus with accurate brevity, "No man should stand in the bight of that sheet!"

The decision is that the turning block was either defective or underdesigned, and that the present circumstances are ideal for making a determination. We set the number five on the opposite tack, explode another turning block, ruin two more stanchions, and probably terminate the useful life of the wire sheet. Before the Bermuda Race, Captain Lawton builds his own turning blocks and beefs up the after rail where they attach. We supernumeraries give the area between block and winch considerable respect. But not enough.

The victim, when disaster strikes, is "Archie," given name Arvid Arnheim, from Oslo, Norway. A traditional yachting hand, "Norwegian Steam" Archie is monosyllabic, massive, and has great, quick hands powerful as vises. He works tirelessly, eats intensely, and thinks with painful deliberation, often standing ponderously still while thought germinates. In the middle of the afternoon, leading the Bermuda fleet, we get a wind shift in about twenty knots of breeze, and tack. Archie, standing a bit too far aft, is caught under the knees by the flailing big genoa sheet, and he is flicked overboard instantly. As quick as he is powerful, he rolls over in midair, clamps both hands on the wire sheet, and is flapped up and down near the cockpit by the flogging jib. Olin Stephens at the helm instantly luffs up, and Corny Shields, then still red-headed and powerful, scoops Archie aboard—but not until the free sheet has opened Archie up along the cheek and temple. Dripping, Archie stands on the deck, the water and the color running out of him simultaneously. He can't swim. The bright blood along his cheek and jaw flares against his pallor, "Ay taut ay vas gone!" he says, very slowly.

We all share a period of silence for the almost departed, realizing yet again, that absolute concentration on what you are doing is the price of successful, and safe, sport.

But in addition to the lethal forces controlled by the smart ocean-going crew, another danger lurks, ready to pounce. Familiarity, skill, practice—all seduce to overconfidence. We watch an outfielder dance across the bright green for the last out, and scoop it out of the air with one hand as he starts for the dugout. It's a gaudy gesture of infinite insolence and skill. Dick Grosmiller sailed a lot with Bill Snaith's *Figaros*, and had that very quality of insolent skill, of making the difficult look casual. It betrayed him, and helped lose us a Fastnet.

Dick was a good cook, a good mechanic, a great helmsman, and a quick sail handler. No one was more willing to bounce on deck at any time, work furiously, leave with a jest, and bounce back for more. We'd taken a close second in the previous Fastnet and were looking good, having sailed through our own class, B, and into class A. It was blowing about eighteen knots southeast, and we were carrying a spinnaker and full main. For rating reasons, we were sailing as a sloop and were trussed 'ıp like a turkey for the oven. The main was vanged and preventered, the spinnaker sheeted and lazy-guyed, with a choker line to the mast to refill it on broaches. It was about 2130, the gloaming in the English Channel, and we had just boiled past the Lizard and headed off for Seven Stones. With the wind now gusting a little and heading us a bit, Bill Snaith opted to shift to genoa. The racket of our hoisting the genoa from the deck got Grossmiller out of the sack, and he appeared on deck in his underpants. Dancing with eagerness, he dashed forward, popped the pin on the spinnaker pole, and started to pull the spinnaker aboard by its skirt, under the genoa. But as the bag was lowered to his hands, a great gust struck us from farther ahead, filled the spinnaker, and yanked Grossmiller off balance. As he let go, he was standing in a mess of spinnaker sheets, and one of them grabbed his leg and ejected him over the rail. In the half dark, he was suddenly a head receding in fifty-five-degree water. We had to get the spinnaker down, cast off vang and foreguy from the main, and tack or jibe to get back to him, all of which would take time.

Bobby Symonette was on the helm, and he immediately gave orders in the clear, persuasive voice that, as speaker, had controlled the Nassau House for many a session. "Norry! Keep him in sight and get a compass bearing on him for as long as you can; you guys get that spinnaker down so that we can beam reach!" We got the spinnaker off, the vang and foreguy released, and at last jibed around and headed back. Seventeen minutes after he went overboard, and well after we'd disappeared over his horizon, we saw him, slightly to leeward, on course. I had made a bowline loop in a sheet, and as we swept alongside Dick, I managed to throw it over his upraised arm and head. He surged aboard at about eight knots, swept water off himself with the edges of both hands, and said, in heartfelt tones, "Boy, am I glad to see you guys!" The feeling was mutual, almost to the point of tears.

His next remark was typically Grossmiller. "Geeze," he said, "we're racing, aren't we? Let's tack the bugger!" And before he went below to dry off (and have a warming belt of whiskey), he got us tacked, vanged, and prevented. We lost the Fastnet again, by six minutes.

I'll never be as dab a hand as Grossmiller because I have too abiding a respect for the unexpected to operate with insolent skill. I prefer deliberate to quick, cautious to gaudy. But a conservative approach does

Grossmiller back aboard shows no strain; R. Symonette, Bucky Reardon, and Bill Cox have not yet recovered.

not necessarily prevent glitches, avoid clumsiness, or achieve perfection. I'm afraid that my personal overboard disasters not only are unexciting, but unfortunately they are amusing to my wife. There was the time, for example, that I carefully got the genoa poled out, the main out against the shrouds, and stepped into the dinghy with a wide angle lens on my Leica to get a picture of the boat. Holding the camera in one hand, I carefully let out line until the whole boat filled the viewfinder. I focused and snapped. And as I snapped, the dinghy came untied, the tow line therefore stopped lifting the bow, and the dinghy dove gracefully beneath the waves. As I treaded water, the camera held high with one hand, Kitty sweetly inquired from the boat (between spasms of giggles), "Now what?" Large problems require stern measures. "Head into the wind!," I screeched. As *Hardtack* ground to a halt, all aback, I sidestroked to her, handed the camera aboard, took down all the sails, started the engine, and went back and retrieved and emptied the dinghy. Through the entire procedure, my bride intermittently tittered, "If you could have seen your face!"

Telling that tale reminds me of our first cruise together with a spinnaker on our thirty-two-foot *Wagtail*. I'd set it successfully off West Chop, and we savored our smooth passage for about an hour until a course change for Nantucket demanded a jibe. I explained the end-for-end jibe to Kitty, jibed the main over, detached the spinnaker pole from the mast, and attached it to the collapsed spinnaker. With both guy and sheet slack, I next intended to poke the pole forward, the spinnaker still collapsed behind the main, detach the inboard end from the spinnaker, attach pole to mast, and then scamper aft and guy the pole back till the bag filled. Alas, the whole operation so fascinated Kitty that she veered to weather and filled the spinnaker while I was crossing the pole. I had a good grip on the middle of the pole as it slowly lifted me into the air above the bow. The pole hit the staysail stay, the spinnaker collapsed as the pole swung, and I came back briskly against the mast. As the spinnaker filled the second time and I again rose, Kitty firmly said, "Norris! Stop that!" By this time I had hit the stay again, rather more briskly, and the pole, off balance, sheered sideways and scraped my hands off it. I shot along the pole and overboard to leeward.

Lightly clothed, it being a hot day, I splashed in ahead of the bow,

Wagtail *with our first spinnaker; Kitty at the helm.*

fended it off with my feet, and was plowed under by the turn of the bilge, emerging, less than pleased, about at the cockpit. The spinnaker pole had now wedged itself into the shrouds, the spinnaker was drawing, and *Wagtail* was heeled down, allowing me to take a grip on the rail and heave myself, fire in my eyes, into the cockpit. Kitty had abandoned the tiller and was peering earnestly forward, about where I'd gone overboard. I grabbed her leg as I slopped into the cockpit, and she spun around to look at me in astonishment. "Oh!" she said. "Thank God! I *wish* you'd be more careful!"

With more patience than I felt, I carefully explained how the maneuver should have gone off, going over several times the general principle that *her* absolute concentration is the price of *my* safety. What I didn't explain is that on little boats, malign forces are only semi-detrimental to humans, praise the Lord. Kitty dined out on frequent retellings of the spectacle of my stately ascent, glaring aft, my hasty return to the mast, and my stately reascent and undignified splash. Her punch line, delivered with wide-eyed, histrionic innocence, was always, ". . . and you should have seen how unreasonable he was when he got back aboard!"

By our third boat, she was as good a helmsman as I've sailed with, thus preserving our marriage, me, and my sense of humor.

10

Oh My Lord!

WHEN THE PHONE RANG, I didn't have a thought in my mind. It was Friday, and my last class of the week was over. "This is Peter Strong," a voice said, "and I wonder if you'd be interested in sailing across the Atlantic?" "When do we leave?" I asked. "Early June," he said, "from Trumpy's yard in Annapolis." "O.K." I said. Peter was not wholly receptive, "Before you make up your mind, we ought to meet each other," he suggested. My mind was made up, but I drove to Andover, where he had finished his last class of the week, and I made up *his* mind. If I ran across a good cook and sailor, I was to sign him on. Our mission was to deliver his father's forty-five-foot Rhodes yawl, *Pavana,* to Norway, where Corrin Strong had just been appointed Ambassador. From a diplomatic point of view, I felt that my immediate acceptance had been undercautious, impolitic, and characteristic. So?

Getting the cook was easy. I asked my favorite sailing companion, Tom Buell, if he wanted the job, and he immediately started to learn cooking from his mother's cook. His first loaf of bread was humorously deployed by his older brother as a doorstop. Tom slowly became more competent.

The crew assembled—Tom, Peter, Bram Arnold (our navigator), Irving Fisk (my watch-mate), and me. We put aboard enough canned goods for two trips, loaded the icebox with a canvas liner and six hundred pounds of Red Ash Anthracite for the number two Shipmate stove. This was on Rod Stephens advice. He thought the trip in a Rhodes yawl would take about twenty-four days. "Don't use anything

Pavana's crew: (left to right) Buell, Arnold, Hoyt, Fisk, Strong (and canary).

but Red Ash Anthracite!" he said. "I know, because my father was a coal dealer." The trip took twenty-four days, and the Red Ash Anthracite lasted exactly twenty-five days, being better planned than the food. We gave away lots of cans in Norway, after cruising three more weeks.

The trip itself was comparatively uneventful. Off the Grand Banks we had a moment of sheer panic when the water suddenly, in the middle of a moonlit night, went chalky bright, as though we were over shallows. Our navigator, secure in his mathematics, turned on the fathometer and got excessive depth. It was melted glacier water, eddying afar. Later, approaching Europe, we picked up the BBC's well-known weather forecasts, and were alarmed with "Tyne, Heligoland, Cromarty, Lundy, gale warnings, force nine, increasing," followed by "Rockall, Irish Sea, hail and gales . . ." Since Bram assured us we were in the Rockall sector, and the wind was already more than two reefs and a spitfire was needed, we set the storm trysail, backed the jib, and hove to. By this time the boat, locally built in the Chesapeake, was working a little. As the gale came on, the hail slashed, and the seas got mountainous, the water began to gain on the available hand pump.

Peter had prepared well, and we had a portable gasoline-driven pump with a two inch I.D. water exhaust and a 2.5-inch I.D. smoke exhaust. Opening a port on the lee side and thrusting both hoses out, we initiated power and watched the water, washing over the floorboards diminish. In due time even the varnished cans, which had been melodiously rolling back and forth in the flooded bilge, went silent. Obviously, from the flow, the source of the leak was in the cockpit area, well blocked off from the cabin by specially built racks of canned goods. Peter made the executive decision, "We'll draw straws to see who goes in by the cockpit hatch." I lost. "Peter," I pleaded, "I can't get through that hatch with my clothes on!" "Norry," he reasonably replied, "then you won't go through it with your clothes on."

The hatch, bronze and circular, was undogged. Wet and cold in "T" shirt and underpants, armed with hose clamps, screwdriver, canvas, grease, needle, thread, and a shot of brandy, I was lowered through the hole between seas, showered as the hatch was returned to position, and abandoned to the task. The lead downcomers from the cockpit drains had pried their solder loose as the ship worked, and every sea that landed in the cockpit drained half its contents into the hull. Eight hose clamps later, we weren't leaking for the nonce, and I howled for escape. We had some minor difficulty getting my knees, which had congealed in a squatting position, through the hatch, but the task was accomplished by major force with minor abrasions.

We landed in Bergen, were joined by Kitty and Peter's cousin, Janet, and with three weeks before the ambassador arrived on the Oslofjord we cruised, filled with the elation of our accomplishment. Conquerors of the fearsome North Atlantic, we admitted our heroic voyage to fellow yachtsmen at dock, club, and anchorage. In Arendal, we were tied astern of a unique vessel. Double-ended and planked in varnished oak, she was of uncertain age, and had been bashed here and there through the years. Her general appearance, cosmetically, was that of a banana contused. We drifted alongside of her and greeted a fine, ruddy-faced old gent, clad in boots with tweedy pants stuffed into them and a heavy shirt with sleeves torn off, which was stuffed into the pants.

Peter Strong, our skipper, and our actor-cook-poet, Tom Buell.

The pants, pleated at the waist, were sustained by sturdy galluses, and above the rubicund face and bald, shining forehead, an explosion of gray hair danced in the breeze. He had a merry eye.

"My name is Balfour," he announced. "Call me Freddie!" We remarked that his yacht certainly looked sturdy, and he led us below for a drink, extracting a bottle of fine scotch from a wine rack under a berth. The cabin sole, covered with linoleum, was grungy, and the frames, revealed by lifting a sodden floorboard, were sawn from enormous lumber and spaced closer than their four-inch breadth. Neat she was not, but she was built for battle!

Fastened on the inside of the cabin trunk I noticed several RORC participation medals. "Ah," I said, "you race!" Freddie replied enthusiastically, "Not to win, y'know, just for sport." "She's a great cruising boat," I blithered. "Have you ever thought of sailing to the United States?" "Ectually," he said, "we hope to, some day. Too much to do right here, now." "Well," I said, "if you sail over, plan to land in Newport. Our house is always open and we can give you showers and wheels." "Splendid!" he replied. Changing the subject, he pointed into the engine compartment. "I supposed you noticed the tub hanging there; my sister mixes gin in it!" We regarded it and him doubtfully. A joke?

Next the party came aboard *Pavana*. Freddie was delighted with the girls, but he was a little dubious about the boat. He looked at the inch-and-a-half frames on ten-inch centers, the half-inch bulkheads, the teak and holly sole. "A bit light, isn't she?" Off Rockall we'd have enthusiastically agreed. Now we answered proudly, "She crossed the Atlantic!" At about this juncture the typical British paid hand came down the dock. He wore a spotless white jump suit, a red canvas hat, and short boots. "Your Lordship," he announced, "the main engine's started." Freddie left after shaking hands all around and offering help and hospitality in Scotland. They disappeared into the channel.

For days thereafter, when I was below, the cockpit resounded with the mirth of my fellows. "I say, Freddie, you rather stink!" "That's tickety boo, old chap; I shall get a bawth at Norry's!"

Eventually, we finished the cruise, replete with incident, got the boat to Oslo, had a party at the embassy, and flew home. Two days after

I got to Newport. I was talking with Houghton Metcalf, who was building his final boat at A & R in Lemweder, Germany. He proposed to cruise Norway with a crew he'd hire in Germany. No worse mistake could be made. In Norway, Quislings' ancestral gravestones are torn from the cemetaries and thrown into the sea. Norwegians, cordial to the whole world, don't answer questions asked by Germans; in fact, do not see Germans. I was earnest with Houghty, and suggested that he hire Scots. I looked up Freddie's address in the RORC yearbook and gave it to him. Freddie, true to his offer, rounded up a splendid pair of seamen and a cook, and Metcalf had a wonderful summer. His last, as it turned out.

Several years later, I sailed across to Cowes with Bill Snaith, took a train to London, and went to the RORC for lunch. I took a fine picture in the cloakroom—four brollies and four derbies hung on four successive hooks. In the dining room, I was greeted by Slim Somerville, then editor of *The Yachtsman*. Slim introduced me to his other guests, a handsome redheaded girl with a Scot's burr to her voice, and her fiancé, a lean, Rudolph Valentino type with a green loden jacket picked out extensively with leather and silver braid. Upon my perhaps undiplomatic inquiry, I found it was the ancestral costume of some very important nobility from a very unimportant area. I transferred my attention to the girl, and was soon merrily telling her the story of Freddie. Somerville enjoyed it immensely. She listened with full attention, many yesses? and thens?, and was not fractured by the punch line about bawths.

"I suppose you realize," she said coolly, "that Lord Balfour is my father."

I may have blanched, but probably not. I instantly realized that her last name was not Balfour, and neither was Freddie's. Lord Byron was, after all, plain George Gordon. "Wait till you hear the rest of the story," I continued. And I built up Houghty Metcalf's last cruise, as rescued from disaster by Freddie. I don't know if she believed me; her fancy fiancé certainly didn't.

A diplomat would never have put in his foot up to the calf like that.

11

Just a Question of Training

I AM WILLING TO ADMIT that women are justifiably jealous of boats. Small wonder. When George McPherson, proprietor of a clutch of hairdressing salons in Los Angeles, became infatuated with the idea of cruising, he personally supervised the construction of his "ultimate" boat in Southampton, a sister ship to Irving Johnson's *Yankee*. Then he had her cabinetry meticulously finished in Holland. Belatedly, he next retrieved his wife from an anti-flesh pôt in Arizona. She had been neglected (and upgraded) for the better part of two years, during which time she had clarified her opinion of boats. She resentfully endured, with George, a cross-continental cruise of canals and rivers, Paris to the Med. The cruise ending, she blasted George's enthusiastic, innocent, and still single-minded question, "Well, love, how do you like her?" "George," she said, "it's me or the boat." Unfortunately, George managed to sell the boat to our friend Moffett before she clarified her opinion of George, and then he had neither!

I confess that boats riveted my attention before girls did, and almost as thoroughly. My spare time, post-puberty, was spent about equally in boatyards and girls' colleges. (In those days we *had* girls' and boys' colleges, so that girls could have a wider choice than co-edu-prison.) I often took my dates on sailing picnics. After a fall of football and a winter of swimming and the library, there was something down-right uplifting about a boat leaning to the wind in the salt spring air.

The company of women was so heady that I reasonably concluded I'd need to find one who could share my enthusiasm for sailing with my enthusiasm for her. To this end, in the summer after my senior year, I took a job with a family that had two sailboats and three daughters, only one of them too young to sail by herself. Unfortunately, having signed for the job in January, I met my future wife in February, thus totally aborting my reasoned approach. Infatuation is not a matter of relative values. Kitty was "tall and queenly, with a terrific left," as a firmly rejected suitor described her. Willingly or not, she got my full concentration.

In those wonder-filled preliminary stages of courtship, as we compulsively told each other our life histories, I learned that she and her sister had owned a sponson sailing canoe in Gibson Island, and that it *would* tip over, if mishandled. They graduated from that to a Snipe, which unlike the canoe, could sink, and was thus more attentively sailed. Their father and uncle together owned, in their youth, a fifty-foot, spoon-bowed, shoal-draft sloop. They summered in Watch Hill, where the water shoaled out at the family dock. The brothers had a favorite trick—they'd come at the dock under full sail on a broad reach, and at the last minute, Uncle John would drop the centerboard and stand on it as Foster dropped the main and jib. The boat would spin in place, halted by the centerboard in the sand. One day they generated more excitement than they intended. The centerboard pennant tangled, and John was standing too high as the boom came over when they hit the dock. All survived.

Concluding from such biographical details that Kitty had a taste for sailing, I intensified my courtship, graduated from Yale, taught for a year, and then, to paper over the holes in my mind, went back to graduate school. Married to Kitty, and with a Ph.D. in English, I took a job as an instructor at Clark University, sixty miles from water. We spent our first spring weekends wandering the coast of New England and looking for a boat the size of our purse. *Hardtack* was twenty-four-feet long, designed and built by Jack Stevens of Goudy and Stevens for his own use. Insured, and fully equipped to Coast Guard regulations, she cost $1,800. I corrected the final exams for my three courses (Chaucer, Milton, and Nineteenth-Century Poetry) while stormbound in York Harbor, Maine, on our delivery cruise to Branford, Connecticut.

Twenty years, two boats, three children, and a dog later, I faced the problem of educating Kitty to new horizons. She was a great cruising mother. But we'd anchored every night, and cruised in New England where we had friends in every port. In general, we had avoided such problems of ocean cruising as lack of company, fatigue, limited supplies, and constricted space. The occasional overnighter is not

Wagtail under full sail, main, spinnaker, diapers, and three children.

preparation for crossing oceans; with three children, we'd had two decades in which we were never alone at sea.

I was acutely aware, after more than twenty years as coach and teacher, that no matter how numerous the lacks or how great the talent, you can teach only one thing at a time. Plainly, the best of my developed skills as a teacher and the very best of equipment were necessary before Kitty and I retired to life on a boat. Singlehanding was out of the question; leaving her as a portrait painting sailing widow for various races, and one cruise across the Atlantic had taught me how eager I was to get home to her. And retirement loomed, fifteen or twenty years down the line.

Our first oceanic educational opportunity came in 1957, when Judge Curtis Bok, with whom I had once voyaged to England, decided to take *Alphard* on the race to Santander, Spain. The victim of a "massive myocardial infarct," he said, rejecting his doctor's severe warning against ocean voyages, "It's less wearing than being rich in Philadelphia." I wrote Kitty into the trip as cook on three counts: better cuisine, a woman's moderating influence, and publicity that would give us prolonged attention and thus diminish danger. Curtis met her and agreed.

It was a great trip. She handled the tight quarters and the limited supplies like a champion, and she was the toast of Santander, graciously receiving, from an elderly Spanish Don, a full armload of calla lilies (suitable for triumph or burial) and a giant silver cup engraved "Ministro de Marine" as "cook on the last boat to finish," an award category created by the immediate circumstances.

O.K., one down, more to go. After all, the trip had been a social triumph, having as companions Curtis, a brilliant judge and author; Redwood Wright, a well-known oceanographer; and Dr. William Lee, one of our ushers and my Yale roommate. Teddy Robbins, the last member of the crew, was a supercompetent youth for the foredeck and a graduate of Princeton's Charm School. The next problem was to see how well an unmitigated diet of me went down. Our boat, a twenty-four-foot S&S Dolphin, had been lent to a friend for three years while I helped deliver the American ambassador's yawl to Norway (Kitty joined us there), and cruised to England with Curtis. In 1958 it became

Kitty cooks and Red Wright cleans glasses on the Race to Spain. Alphard,
1957.

ours again, and Kitty and I, for the first time in more than twenty years, had a chance to cruise Maine alone together. We brought the boat back from the boatyard in Sorrento (which victimized me as a $ummah Vi$itah), and had a delightful three weeks in those pine-scented, lobster-buoyed waters. On the second day out, I nearly blew my whole game plan down the tube. We were sailing off Mt. Desert Bar when an enormous, black thundersquall bore down on us. I hastily got down and lashed the sails and pushed the starter button. Nothing happened. I dashed below to reason with the engine; Kitty bore off before the rising wind, under bare poles, the sky green-black to boom level, with the late afternoon sun blasting through beneath. Enormous hail fell. To avoid being brained, Kitty grabbed a sponge-rubber cockpit cushion and put it over her head. The falling hail, big as pullet eggs, bounced off the cushion and met the falling hail still descending. A halo of shattered ice, backlighted, appeared around her as she yelled for relief and pulled her hands out of the line of fire. Focusing deliberately, I got a tremendous picture; I was not immediately forgiven. She had to admit, however, that our pair-bonding was not shallow. Later, I'm afraid, she "lost" the picture.

The engine never did start. Our son, Wm. B., drove the car up so that Kitty could drive back to do a portrait painting commission.* Wm. B. remained with me. Merle Hallett's yard found the key to the problem, and we got the boat to Newport in easy stages and sold it. Kitty was positive it wasn't big enough for prolonged habitation.

While we mulled means and choice of a live-aboard cruising boat, I spent the next thirteen summers either broadcasting the America's Cup from Newport or crossing the Atlantic on *Kormoran, Cyane, Ondine, Xanadu II, Kytra II, Passagemaker, Solution, Figaro, Kay, Linnet, Carina,* or *America,* Kitty accompanying me on *Kytra II* and *Passagemaker.* Meanwhile, having completed my twenty-five years as chairman of the St. George's English Department (5.5 subordinates), I became a senior master, a position which carried with it a year off

---

*Christened "Newport's Foremost Necrodelineator" by her children, Kitty has painted, among others, portraits of deceased dedicatory personages for the Wilkinson Library, the Dyer Geriatric Wing of Newport Hospital, Miss Lucy Aldrich (commissioned by her brother, The Honorable Winthrop, Chairman of the Museum of Modern Art), The Senior Citizens Center, and several others. She does live children better, and by preference.

(with salary) while the new chairman had his own unobstructed way. I called my friend, Guy Goodbody, and offered to deliver his fifty-foot, one-off, Angus Primrose cold-molded sloop, *Kytra II*, from Scotland to Malta, where he could join us. He was enthusiastic.

Since the boat had been designed for the single-handed Transatlantic Race, here was an opportunity to test, with perfect equipment, our ability to manage a ship together, resist fatigue, and handle the stresses of ocean cruising. Our first stress was on shore and was financial. While Goodbody and I were stormbound in Oban, in Scotland, Kitty and our younger daughter, Minnie, arrived on schedule at the Royal Marine Hotel at Dunlaoghaire (pronounced *dun leary*) and enjoyed luxurious breakfasts in bed. For three days, BBC's marine weather broadcast was "Tyne, Heligoland, Cromarty, Lundy, force nine; Fastnet, Irish Sea, hail and gales . . ." We waited. Finally, we made the wonderful transit of the Irish Sea, where the tide fills and ebbs from both ends, so you can carry it all the way. Goodbody bade us farewell at the Royal Irish Yacht Club, and as is traditional with international voyagers, we gave all our Irish coinage to the club boatman before we set sail for Finisterre.

Min was prostrated by *mal-de-mer* with qualms all the way, so Kitty and I found ourselves coping with solitary watches, an active galley, and an unknown boat. By the time we beat in against a half gale through the Straits of Gibraltar, we had total confidence in each other. In the following months, we worked out several useful patterns. At Kitty's insistence, we rented a tiny house in Malta and found ourselves in the local social stream—until spring. The ocean racing I had done found old shipmates at quay and yacht club wherever we subsequently sailed. We branched out from there. Cruising east, Kitty suggested we telephone friends to join us, and thus injected their varieties of tastes and backgrounds into our patterns. We made new acquaintances dockside, and exchanged charts from where they'd been east for charts we'd covered west. As members of CCA, we were eligible to see (and Xerox) the private information sheets of RCC members, which tell, for each

OVERLEAF: *Guy Goodbody's* Kytra II *off Korcula, Yugoslavia.*

harbor diagram, where previous cruisers have been well treated or
cheated. We digested Denholm and Pilkington and annotated then
with glue-in flimsies filled with information from recent cruisers. All in
all, as we sailed to each new horizon, we managed an endless sense of
anticipation.

Minnie, disenchanted with sailing by a month of woopsing, went
to school at Tal Handaq, the British Military's Malta establishment,
while she boarded and worked at a riding academy in the spring term.

One development worried me. Kitty frequently disappeared when
we were ashore together. In Greece, where most of the shops open into
one another and then into back streets, she'd shop endlessly. Drifting
from counter to counter, musing about value and suitability, to me
seems as unrewarding as bridge or chess, where complex intellectualiza-
tion has no tangible result. Eventually, I learned to let her dive into
shops while I sat under the mimosas, watched people, sipped ouzo,
noshed bits of fried octopus, and coped with an uneasy sense of having
been abandoned by talking to strangers. On one occasion, she drifted
off the boat while we were fueling. I assumed she was below. Our guests
and I took off, and I missed her almost thirty minutes later. We
returned at max-rpm, scanning the wild waves all the way. Amid the
ha-has and ho-hos of our relieved reunion, I resisted the impulse to
examine the role of my retaliatory subconscious in this episode.

When my sabbatical year ended, we returned to Newport and
teaching, but we agreed that we'd retire to a life of cruising aboard a
suitable boat. In my mind there was only one question, "What boat?"
It was 1972, and the school was getting a new headmaster. I could retire
with social security in three years, and we had moved into lesser digs
from the grandeur of our department head's house. We could put
about $50,000 into a boat and still have a marginally livable income.
At this point Kitty came on strong. "I hope you don't think we can
just go cruising," she said, "without disposing of sixty years of accumu-
lation." "Boats don't get taxed," I ominously grouched. "Houses are
at the mercy of political spending." But I agreed that we had to have
a house. We possessed furniture, thousands of books, clothes, pictures,
and (at the time) two unmarried daughters. Had I painstakingly, over
long years, trained Kitty for a nonexistent role? Could we ocean cruise
on a smaller boat?

History contributed toward a partial solution to our problem. Rhode Island, a small state extensively indebted to the Democrats, was alone in rejecting Nixon. Nixon reciprocated by pulling the Democratic goodies out of Rhode Island, which meant the loss of millions in Navy salaries at Quonset, Charlestown, Newport Naval Base, and the War College. In Newport in the tight downtown streets, the small houses which had been cut into wee apartments that had rented for $300 a month lost their tenants. Real estate agents doubled their files, and dwellings that had been passed from swabbie to swabbie since 1941 came on the market, many of them at the price they'd gone for in 1939.

I suggested to Kitty that $10,000 of the boat fund would be enough for a two-room cottage. A day later, she trapped me after class and took me into Newport. The house she had found had two apartments of three rooms each, plus a kitchen and a bath in each apartment. The attic had two bedrooms and a closet (for us); the dirt-floor cellar had a furnace that belonged in the National Archives. In one apartment, recently abandoned by three sailors, the four walls were completely filled, except for windows and doors, with hundreds of kinds of empty beer cans, neatly stacked, floor to ceiling. Further furnishings, which we were able to give away to a junk man, came with the house. The price was $11,500; I wrote a check. The roof needed reshingling. The covering on the B-X cable dissolved and fell upon contact. Stoves, refrigerators, and radiators worked fine.

We gave Katy the first floor and took the rest, moved in, persuaded the school to grant us $600 a month for rental, and hired Paul, Minnie's friend, to rewire us. I gave him shirts upon which I had silk-screened a circular lightning stroke that enclosed the gothic-lettered title, "Short Circle Elec. Corp." Two months rent paid Paul and three months rent paid the roofing expert. The final problem the house posed was space; the rooms, about ten by fourteen, built just after 1800 by "Bacchus Overing, black certified insane," wasn't going to hold us, our furniture, and tons of books.

Our son took the excess furniture. I built bookcases along the outside walls and filled them, built bookcases around the furnace in the cellar (in some summers, everything in Newport has a need to mildew), and ended with about two pick-up loads of books. After trying to give these to libraries and Episcopal Salvage, I left them in the school halls for grabs, and finally ended up transporting the more solemn (*Bibliography of English Literature*, etc.) to the dump, where they rapidly became nondeductible.

I felt the last roadblock had been cleared. Kitty was aligned with the future, and the horizon looked bright. I had a house, a first mate, ready money, employed children, and all necessary skills. Then, that next spring, after I helped my good friend Bob Gunther bring his forty-one-foot sloop up from Florida, he sold it to me for its company-depreciated value, which came very close to my budget. In the ensuing summer, Kitty and I circumnavigated New England, via the Hudson River, Lake Champlain, the Richlieu, and the St. Lawrence. The boat passed all tests. We returned to Newport wholly willing to adopt a cruising life together, with Kitty's additions of a nest, friends to join us, and the occasional shoreside rental. I informed the school I was retiring and began buying books on world cruising. "Here we go!" I told her.

"Darling," she said, "it's been a struggle, but I think, at last, I've managed to train you for it."

12

The Engine and I

I HAVE ALWAYS FELT AT EASE with engines, pressing their starters with assurance, feeling their thrust with a full heart, approving their little, intimate noises under their strong, regular rhythm. In The War (W.W. II, *our* war), I even got the second highest grades in Diesel Engineering at Fort Snafu, having been bested only by Harold Stassen (who never made connection with effective machinery thereafter). So, when we bought *Telltale II* and plotted world cruising, I thought in terms of a crash review on her five-year-old diesel, a shakedown cruise to work out stowage, procedures, and personnel management (my wife, guests)—and thence off to blue horizons.

Our shakedown cruise would circumnavigate New England by way of Sing-Sing Prison (Hudson River, Lake Champlain, St. Lawrence River, Nova Scotia, and home). The course would provide hot and cold, fresh and salt, fog and fair, hardscrabble and hedonism. An all-in-all.

My plans went like butter. I spent a day at the Westerbeke plant and learned everything (it seemed) that could result from mistreatment of a diesel, how to attack problems, and how to cure them. I acquired the owner's guide, the service bulletins, and the mechanic's guide. I read them through and recoiled in surprise at some things I'd never done (and no disaster yet), and developed an aggravated consciousness of the complexity of the iron mainsail. Unfortunately, this consciousness excited my excellent memory, and I subsequently found myself waking at 0400 in our Newport bedroom, an imaginary diesel clanking in anguish, and the box wrench too fat to fit between stud and casting. The current ran relentlessly, the mast lay perilously in cradles six feet above the deck, and the Hudson's wind and waves were rising. "Dreams," I told myself, as I brushed midnight out of my teeth and went back to sleep, "go by opposites." Sloping off in slumber, I considered having the engine thoroughly overhauled. It would have been a good thing.

With Dick, Margot, and Holly Grosvenor along, we happily steamed out of Newport on June 15th, only two hours behind schedule. (Always schedule departures for Sunday noon, when stores are closed and The Girls can't disappear on A Final Mission.) Under sail and/or power, we attended parties at Stonington, Sachem's Head, Southport, and Oyster Bay. At Oyster Bay I had my first opportunity to put my comprehensive knowledge to use. The raw water pump developed a drizzle from under its middle area, which I instantly analyzed as a broken water seal. In a trice I had the belt removed, and three wrenches and a barked knuckle later, had the item in my hand. It had worked long and faithfully, but the seal had gone, and the bearings had followed it. The whole rotated freely and made a grinding, rattling noise. The book said a new pump cost $90, a telephone call located one, and a borrowed car got it. It went on easily, and gave me an inflated sense of competence.

In this first year of my ownership, the motor was reluctant to start, and shifted stiffly. Not wanting to hurt the manufacturer's feelings, I had not mentioned these weaknesses in my crash course, and being politically slightly to the right of Rutherford B. Hayes, I see no need for change in anything that more-or-less works. On a perfect day, we caught a good breeze out of Oyster Bay, sailed to Hell Gate where it died, and motored with boiling currents past Manhattan. We set sail and carried the tide out past the Statue of Liberty, lost the wind, started the engine before we were swept out of the Narrows and motored hard against the current to the slack along the Jersey shore. A gentle breeze came in and increased, until we were swept up the Hudson, wing and wing, to Tarrytown. There, at the entrance to the narrow, shallow channel leading to the marina, we started the engine and maneuvered into a slip next to Lawrence Rockefeller's motorboat.

A splendid meal on board, a long walk and ice cream ashore, and a watercoloring expedition into the hills next morning brought around a flooding current, and we prepared to cast off for the short run to West Point. I pressed the starter button in bland confidence and got a dull click. A wrench on the starter's backside wouldn't turn it. So it wasn't a stuck Bendix. I took it off. The fit was close, but a sturdy heave brought it free on the run, where a bolt head, impacting my index finger between starter and bolt, gave me a nasty cut. Bleeding freely, I ruefully contemplated a starter that was almost a solid mass of rust. Why it had worked for the last two years was an ineluctable mystery. A call to the manufacturer, an Avis car to Stamford where the replacement was located, hollow laughter from the dealer when the suggestion of an allowance for the (rebuildable?) old starter was mentioned, and $193 had us back aboard. The engine started with unprecedented energy and enthusiasm. I basked in expertise.

The Hudson was wonderful to us. An obliging twenty-knot wind from astern kept us cool and gave us eight knots on course. We found ready anchorages, moorings, and marinas, had our mast laid down in Catskill, and progressed famously to Albany. Next morning, the gear-shift refused to function, and now, gun-shy from previous mechanical malaise, I diagnosed the worst without looking—the reverse gear was bonkers.

From this first erroneous assumption, I backed myself into the "Mistake of the Trip." I used a telephone number on the wall of the Albany Yacht Club to get a diesel mechanic, and I told him we had clutch trouble. Arriving from the Brockhurst Trucking Company, he immediately sensed that I was an idiot (the gearshift cable had seized up), and after prolonged poking around, took out the cable and shifted the engine easily. Then, assuring me that a replacement cable would be forthcoming shortly, he disappeared. After he'd been gone two hours, I found that Brockhurst was within walking distance of the boat. The vast garage, which was empty of trucks, was filled with foremen, supervisors, bookkeepers, typists, telephone operators, and supernumerary personnel. In two more hours the truck and mechanic reappeared, assuring us that no such cable was available in Albany. I picked up a nearby telephone, significantly, and managed to order one sent ahead c.o.d. from the manufacturer. I was then billed seventy-one dollars for the mechanic's time (which had been spent trailing around town in search of a Morse cable whose number he could have communicated by phone), plus fifty cents a mile for the use of the company truck. The service manager was about seven feet tall and three hundred pounds on the hoof so, laughing nervously and making good-fellow noises, I paid. For eighty-two dollars and minor mental anguish, I had learned further rules for dealing with the iron mainsail:

1) Never tell a mechanic what you think; just report symptoms.

2) Give him full-court coverage, basketball style; you may know more about the Yellow Pages than he does.

3) Messages on the walls of public conveniences are not guarantees of integrity.

4) A delegate in the engine room can shift gears, even all the way to Burlington.

The cruise continued to be a delight. Mast in cradles now, we went up the Champlain Canal with the engine humming cheerfully and cows, cottages, marinas, and monuments passing placidly beside us. As we drilled along, sketching pictures of Victorian lighthouses and each other, we remembered the admonition to keep watching the engine panel—vigilance there is labor saved later. There was a gentle current against us, and by late afternoon the engine was running about ten degrees warmer than its Hudson average. At Schuylerville, dockside, I closed the through-hull intake, cleaned eelgrass and gurry out of the intake water strainer, and noticed that its gasket had been seeping. With four artists aboard (and me), we had lots of good paper, and I cut a gasket out of a heavy sheet of Arches, got the strainer back together, and snugged it down. At about this point a rented car arrived, and we took off for a tour of Saratoga and dinner. The boat started perfectly well the next morning with the through-hull valve closed, but it wasn't long before the engine-panel-watch had dehydration to howl about.

The enormity of my oversight was slow in registering. I knew the drill. We cut the engine off. Then we put the rubber dinghy overboard, installed the outboard, and pushed the boat along at three knots. I dove into the engine, took the faceplate off the raw water pump, dug out the fragments of the impeller, and assembled them for a head count.

I was missing most of two blades. Off with the oil cooler. A bit of digging and back blowing got out all but bitty fragments, which the cooling system could pass quite easily. I put the cooler back, went forward to the engine spares, and brought back a spare impeller. The wrong size! And so were the other two!

I filed the impeller's shaft hole to fit the shaft, put discs of inner tube on both sides of the housing to flesh out the hole, and installed the impeller, feeling as clever as a home-improvement writer for *Woman's Day*. But it didn't work.

The last resort of the desperate mechanic is his wife's address book. Friends lived only forty miles away, close to the super-competent Shelburne Marina. Armed with complete statistics, they managed to arrive for cocktails and dinner, having gotten a suitable impeller, which I found a superb, nonalcoholic stimulant. Unfortunately, come the dawn, the engine still overheated, and we limped our way through the last lock and out into Lake Champlain at three knots. Buoy 7 Marina had, we were told, the best mechanic on the lake. I had lost faith in my own infallibility.

The great mechanic was an elderly, ironic gentleman, who heard my confession, looked wordlessly at the engine, and told me to bring the exhaust manifold, the elbow, and the Aqualift into the shop. When I had thus disassembled them, he poured a violent, smoking Dr. Jekyll mix into their rusty areas, and lo and behold, openings appeared where only seepage had been before. Flushed with lots of fresh water and re-connected to a scrubbed-out exhaust manifold and Aqualift, the engine cooled elegantly. Rust formed in salt water swells as it soaks in fresh water and blocks passage. Neither owner's nor mechanics' manuals mention this phenomenon.

So now the engine, as it turned out, was cured of five years of age and casual use—elegantly efficient, docile, reliable, the epitome of a carefree diesel.

But carefree I was not. Repeated trauma had made me apprehensive and engine-goosey. The next episode in the engine saga came at midnight in the Northumberland Strait, with the shoals of Prince Edward Island on one side and the Shoals of Richibucto on the other. It was blowing a gale and raining when the mainsail blew out. By the

time I got the storm trysail up, our position was doubtful. By the time
I located where we were and needed the engine, it started, ran briefly,
and quit utterly. Bleeding the engine, grinding the starter, exhortation,
and prayer were unavailing. Twelve hours later, we sailed into Char-
lottetown, where Hurricane Blanche distracted us and the local popula-
tion for the next twenty-four hours. Two mechanics later, the engine
was partially disassembled and no solution was in sight. In desperation
I was sent to another master mechanic, Horace Cameron, two years
retired, who contributed, enginewise, to my further education.

By telephone, he had no inclination to consider my problem. This
line exhausted, I drove out to his house and talked of other things,
drank his coffee, and offered to deliver the high pressure pump to his
test bench. That got him. "Don't take anythin' off the engine till I've
seen it," he said. His reaction to the fragmented engine was brief. "Put
all that back together," he said. "I'm goin' to get some ether." On his
return, he had me pour a quarter cup of fuel into the air intake. He
poured ether on his hanky and held it over the intake, and he pressed
the button. The engine zipped into life, ran briefly, and died as before.
Professor Cameron made his third and final comment of the day, "Find
the air leak; I'm goin' home."

An hour of painstaking research produced no air leaks. Finally I
took the pump for the inflatable, connected it to the fuel tank air vent,
and pumped a pressure in the tank, all on the theory that you can't see
a leak *in,* but you can see a leak *out.* But nothing spouted fuel. As a
last, despairing gesture, I started the engine, and it caught, ran true and
sweet, and went on running. Like daybreak, revelation filled my soul.
I tried blowing out through the detached air vent, and I couldn't; it
was blocked by who knows how many eons of dried, salt spray!

When Horace Cameron returned, the engine was rolling cheerfully, rebuilding the depleted battery. He was gratified. He refused pay
on the ground that he hadn't been working, just teaching. A retired
teacher myself, I accepted his animadversion without comment, and
enjoyed the strong, regular rhythm of my red friend in the basement.

But it will take me a long time to recover mechanical complacence.
The capstone to the summer came off Portland, some fifty engine hours
later. The engine wouldn't start, and I dashed for the toolbox. My wife

pushed in the fuel cutoff with which one stops the engine, pressed the starter, and smiled sardonically at me as I emerged, astonished, from the after cabin. I felt unfaithful.

In essence, my neglect, mistreatment, and ignorance had been responsible for the whole complex of problems, and I'd lost faith in my red friend. I apologize, my friend. I'll get a licensed doctor of motors to give you a complete checkup, then I'll correct the simple things and avoid exploratory openings. And in the minutes between putting out the light and giving myself over to the soft tide of sleep, I'll think, "It isn't the engine; it's the maintenance," and I won't count sheep.

13

Three of a Kind

WHEN I WAS YOUNG, which was more than a few years ago, it was my ambition some day to write a vastly entertaining autobiography in which all my stupid mistakes and disasters eventuated in triumph. At the age of seventy, moderate maturity brought the realization that mistakes are much more entertaining, even to the victim, than triumphs. The Good Lord in his wisdom has added to the human mix such a generous measure of ineptitude, as a bond between people, that it takes a real boob to be self-important, an idiot to be pompous.

Thus we normal people, granted that sense of justice that allows us to slough off failures as educational, can view our inexplicable asininities as discoveries, our illogical relating of fact with fact as research. For example, three exceedingly intense experiences have caused me always to cross my arms across my chest when I'm cold. It all started with an adiabatic reaction.

An adiabatic reaction is a fact of weather. When a cold air mass shovels under a warm, moist air mass, it pushes the warm air up. But when anything causes warm, moist air to rise, the warm air encounters lower temperatures, and saturated air is always on the edge of precipitation. Now, for every ounce of water precipitated from humid air, eighty calories of heat are released, and, as we all know (don't we, students?), hot air rises. As it rises, more precipitates. Ha! It starts going up so fast it pulls in more moist air from the bottom, begins to accelerate toward its source of moisture, and in the Northern Hemisphere, it begins to twist clockwise. This reaction, combined with centrifugal force, generates an even bigger suction than the adiabatic reaction, and motion

known as the Coreolis Effect. The end product, as I understand it, of
all that air adiabatting and coreolling, is one hell of a breeze, ranging
from a squall to a tornado or a hurricane, all brothers under the cloud.
Sailors, caught in one of these excesses of nature, must cope.

I was crewing for George Washington Blunt White on his forty-
three-foot yawl, *White Mist*, in a race from Stamford to the Vineyard
Lightship and back—about 300 miles. With a two-mast availability to
set lots of light sails, we'd made great competitive time downwind in
Long Island Sound, managed a brilliant light air windward effort when
we got a shift off Fisher's Island, and rounded the Vineyard well ahead
of our class and with a few tailenders in "A" tucked away. The wind
shift gave us hope that we could do even better going home, and we
carried the spinnaker, pole on stay, inside Block Island, tidal predictions
giving us a couple knots through the constriction between the island
and Point Judith. Then it clouded up, and a squall line appeared ahead
near Charlestown when we saw it. So we dropped the bag, went to the
big genoa, strapped her in, and started to work our way west. The squall
line turned blacker, Blunt got all hands at the alert, and as the preliminary gusts came in, we shifted to the working jib. The squall was a
whamdoozer—it put the rail under, caused the helmsmen to give the
wheel full turns and every bit of his muscle, and nevertheless broached
us up to a luff several times. The main needed a reef, the rain was falling
in buckets, and all hands were playing the first act of "A Storm at Sea"
with resigned apprehension. As usual, the reel winch for the main
halyard was on the low side of the mast, and as usual, I found myself
there. Blunt had the reefing outhaul on a winch to weather and was
yelling at me to "Get the God damned thing down, what the hell is
holding things up!," etc! I had the brake off, and the handle in two
hands, but the halyard was plainly jammed in the masthead sheave.
Letting go with one hand as *White Mist* went into her third broach,
I smacked the handle smartly with the other and the halyard let go,
snatching the handle out of my other hand and giving me a smart blow
on the cheekbone. My cheek went numb, my instinctive reaction had
thrown the brake shut again, and Blunt, ritually profane for the sheer
dash of it, inquired, "What the hell is wrong now?" There was a great
deal of red on my rain gear, and tentatively feeling my cheek, I encoun-

tered a hole big enough for three fingers, in which there were no teeth. Realizing the aperture was not my mouth, I peered around the mast and said, "Blunt, I think I'm hurt."

"Hurt," he said, "Jesus Christ, You're killed! Don't bleed on my sail!"

I have fast reaction times, so I'd only severed the facial artery. After futile attempts to stop the flow (a tourniquet around my neck made me faint), we abandoned a race we looked to have won. I felt terribly guilty, as Frank Norton drove Nicky Brown and me to the hospital.

Newport is a great place for facial surgery because Newport surgeons get lots of practice patching together sailors who, having fallen asleep while driving to duty for dawn muster, have rammed their cars into the telephone poles at the curb on West Main Road. Dr. Adelson, the father of one of my students, let out my cheek like a mink pelt, and pinned it to my jaw to heal. The scar is almost invisible, but the operation had an unexpected result. My cheek nerves ended downhill, in my mouth. So whenever I eat ice cream, my left cheek feels very chill and numb.

Now ice cream is a special treat for sailors because, unless your boat has a deep freezer, you spend a lot of time without it. Cruising with the children, the post-dinner expedition ashore for ice cream was our happiest ritual. We never had a better time eating ice cream than during the '54 hurricane in Marion.

We had gone to the Ice Cream Parlor there and had maple-walnut ice cream all around, the two older children having two scoops each. Minnie, aged two, could only polish off one. We were awakened the next morning at about seven by the launch boy, who told us that it was predicted to blow quite hard, and who suggested we shift to a mooring. He recommended the one ahead of us, well out near the harbor mouth, which held, when she was there, a ninety-four-foot steel Rhodes motor-sailer. Its two massive mooring pennants barely made it through the chocks on either side of our bowsprit, and with old docking line, I parceled them against chafing on our chain bobstay. By ten o'clock, the wind was at forty, and the harbor was a froth of waves and pitching boats. Kitty instituted a game of "I doubt it!" with the children, and I patrolled the deck in heavy boots and rain gear.

As hurricanes went, Hurricane Carol was a winner. The tide rose as high as the downstairs windows of the houses along the waterfront; unattended boats began to come loose and tack across the harbor (at least those who had severed rather than dragged their anchors). I watched one boat sail exactly between two building sheds and wedge itself upright and unharmed. Three elderly gents aboard a fifty-five-foot schooner waved nonchalantly to us as their boat broke loose, was turned downwind, and sailed into the woods at the foot of the harbor until the trees stopped her. Our dinghy, tied astern, flapped from the water to ten feet in the air until its painter broke and it flipped and cartwheeled out of sight. Meanwhile, the sod and shrubbery of the island at the harbor head came loose and fled by us, the screen doors and back doors of houses flipped erratically side over side down the harbor, and boat after boat went ashore and, clearing sunken stone walls, embosked itself in trees that were tossing and shedding leaves and limbs. All the folding chairs in the yacht club floated down harbor, and as the wind shifted, they came back. I retrieved three.

During the worst of the storm, I spent my time lying on the bowsprit, pelted with spray like birdshot, and renewing the parceling on the pennants. On one trip aft as I crawled on hands and knees to get more line, the wind lifted me clear of the deck and spun me around against my hastily shifting grip on the handrails. Kitty fed the kids and played "I doubt it!" and watched the ports for my feet.

The bravest sight I saw was a N. Y. 32 that dragged into the swamp and grounded, broadside. They reefed down to the numbers as the seas broke over them, and when the wind shifted, they sailed back out, heeled almost horizontal with wind abeam and spray slashing flat to leeward, rounded up, and managed to get another anchor down and achieve stasis.

When the storm had passed, at about five thirty in the afternoon, I swam ashore with our oars, appropriated a dinghy that was upside down in someone's ruined garden, and came back to the boat. It was time to look around for ours; the kids had had more than enough of sandwiches and "I doubt it!" We took the three chairs with us and left them on the Yacht Club lawn, as many other people were doing. Folk from all over the harbor were returning itinerant cans of unlabeled paint to the boatyard. But the prize of the day was at the Ice Cream Parlor—all you can eat at a nickle a scoop! The electricity was out, of course, and the freezer had a limited expectancy. We pigged out joyously, three ecstatic children and their exhausted parents. Dinghies were lined up for blocks on the sidewalk, but not ours. Someone took us back to *Wagtail*.

We sailed slowly home, visiting Padanarum where the harbor ended ashore. Harry Morgan's *Djinn*, and *Malay*, the Bermuda Race Winner of earlier summer, were ashore; *Malay* with her back and mast broken across the bridge; the Concordia Yard's collection was all along the waterfront street—it was depressing. And so was Quisset. It was tragic.

We went back to our mooring in Newport. Newport had had a fairly moderate time. We went home, our summer cruising over. Exactly one week later there were hurricane warnings, this time predicting the center would pass right over Newport. Having worried about the family for one hurricane, I was not about to risk anybody in the second, so I stripped the boat of everything on deck, stowed all but the mainsail below, took the (substitute) dinghy home, and laced and lashed lots of line around the mainsail cover. She was on a 250-pound mushroom, with two pennants, which I lashed to the end of the ten-inch square oak bowsprit, where they couldn't chafe against the chain bobstay. *Wagtail* lasted through the first three hours of the hurricane. But come the calm, and then the initial blast of almost 100-mile-an-hour winds from the opposite direction, everything left in the harbor flipped its mushroom anchors and dragged toward the south shore. *Wagtail* dragged inevitably in toward the sea wall at Harbour Court, John Nicholas Brown's Norman manor house on the waterfront. Police, on emergency duty and stationed all along the waterfront to prevent looting and sacrificial heroism, wouldn't let me near the boat. It grounded on the Browns' abandoned cast-iron sewage outfall, broke it, and was pinned by a pointed shard ten feet off the sea wall, saved by a fluke from being smashed to kindling, as two other yachts already had been. Near *Wagtail*, a forty-eight-foot steel Zodiac ketch was resonantly attacking the Browns' stone dock.

By four thirty in the afternoon the storm had passed. It was low, low tide, and *Wagtail* lay on her side, full of water, with a hole pierced in her by a timber that had caught between boat and seawall. If I could patch the hole and pump her, I could save her, so I got police permission and went aboard. Her forehatch had been washed ashore. Under it I put all my clothes, including shoes and socks, except for underpants and T-shirt. It was hot.

My first move was to carry a line from the bow to the outer cleat on the Browns' dock; then I took the anchor, tied about thirty feet of line to it, buoyed it, and threw it overboard astern. Diving in, I went down, picked up the anchor, and carried it into deeper water. I did that about thirty times, finally getting it fifty yards into the harbor. I attached an anchor rode to it and brought that back to *Wagtail*'s cockpit. Now, with the anchor winch and the cockpit winches, I turned the awash boat over its keel, and got the holed plank out of water on the high side. With canvas, plywood, goombah, and Anchorfast nails, I patched it. Next I baled all I could with a bucket, cleaned the kiddies' comic books (forbidden, but hidden aboard) out of the bilge pump, and pumped her dry. By the time the tide rose and floated her, I had fetched a new battery, had thoroughly rinsed and dried the distributor and starter in the boat's oven, and had clean, dried, and reinstalled the spark plugs in dry cylinders with a teaspoon of ether in each cylinder.

Once afloat, I cast off the Browns' dock, pulled out to the anchor, raised the mainsail, pulled up the anchor, and sailed around till I found an empty mooring, to which I made fast.

By this time it was eleven o'clock at night, Newport was totally dark, what with the electrical poles being down all over, and I was wet, cold, tired, and very pleased with myself. The engine had started, run riotously at first, and then steadied down to a proper rumble. I ran it until it stopped emitting steam from every crevice, cut it, and swam ashore. A kind friend had thoughtfully carried all my clothes home!

St. George's School, where we had a faculty house on campus, was three miles away. In wet underpants and T-shirt and barefoot, I jogged home. I felt almost nothing but hard pavement and shivers, but when I joined my welcoming family they exclaimed in astonishment, "What have you done to yourself?" while looking at my chest. I had worn both nipples raw while jogging home, and was bleeding into my shirt.

I had to wear bandages on my bosom for a week, and aroused a certain amount of rude laughter among my closer friends. Oddly enough, to this day, whenever I'm cold, I fold both hands across my bosom and cover the key points with my hands.

14

Strange Bedfellows

WHEN ONE OCEAN RACES, everything counts. Having been on *Crusade* when she lost the Fastnet because a retired naval person only timed finishes to the minute, and on *Figaro* when she took second for the fourth time in the Fastnet because we were becalmed outside Plymouth and watched the winner catch up with us and follow us in with the newly turned tide, I'm more than aware that seconds count. I do not, therefore, look quizzically at my skipper when he puts me to bed at anchor, rows out into the harbor, and shifts the beddings around on each tack until the boat is balanced on her lines. He may save seconds, later to waste them, of course, in slow or overeager sail changes, navigational options, or failure to purchase a second light spinnaker.

Inevitably, having the boat perfectly balanced means that, on the wind, most of the crew will be sleeping hot bunks on the weather side, even if elsewhere there are enough for all. Downwind, the crew moves aft. So you climb into a recently vacated bunk arranged by someone with different sleep habits. If the upholstery is plastic, I like to put a blanket, hospital cornered, between me and the plastic, and then super-impose the sheet. I feel straitjacketed in a sleeping bag, and therefore I like it on top of me, not surrounding me. At sea, with a good sea running, I also like as much adventitious baggage as possible in the bunk with me, to wedge me into a lengthwise package, immovable in the romp and tumble of the waves.

In my many years of long races, it has always been my habit to carry a full complement of cameras—earlier at least four cameras (fast and

slow black and white, fast and slow color), and lenses from wide angle
to telephoto, close-up to fisheye. Two bricks of film will generally cover
a summer, possibly three. This load of *équipe* used to pose problems
with owners not used to me. At the end of the summer, I always dove
into the darkroom for a couple of weeks of late nights, and made up
a book of 100 eight by ten pictures, mounted and bound, for each
member of the crew. Thus my junk was acceptable to Those Who
Knew, but a skipper deeply concerned with weight, and a bunkmate
who might find two bags of cameras uncomfortable, made it wise for
me to arrive at the boat while everyone was shopping or eating, secrete
my cameras, and reappear later with my clothing. To realize the seri-
ousness of this less than honest approach, conceive, if you can, Skipper
Shorty Trimingham refusing to let his crew carry sea boots (four
pounds a pair) for the ice-cold waters of the English Channel!

If it were possible to choose one's bunkmate, then pre-race pro-
gramming of his responses might make everything simple, but it generally is not. If the boat is large enough to have a navigator for each
watch, for example, the off-watch navigator will share a bunk with the
on-watch navigator. Ditto the cooks-designate. And since you only
meet your bunkmate aboard, the problem can be intimidating.

I was never more intimidated than in the 1969 Fastnet, when I was
the alternate navigator to Admiral Ray McCaig, in Sir Max Aitken's
Crusade. Being an admiral requires an ability to turn on the frost when
it's necessary to deny the sunshine of a smile. As an ex-Lt. Jr. Grade
in the U.S. Naval Reserve, I have a powerful built-in reflex impulse to
salute, genuflect, or hide whenever I see more than two-and-a-half
stripes. As an ex-PT skipper, I had never been in that area of the Navy
where admirals were a localized species. And there I was, in unfamiliar
waters, a totally amateur naviguesser with a sea bag and two bags of
cameras. Introduced, I greeted him warily, trying to convey (in my
best low-key manner) extreme competence, willingness to adapt, and
loyalty-up.

McCaig was tall, lean, dark, and equipped with a marvelous smile

Sir Max Aiken at the helm of Crusade.

Admiral McCaig in Crusade's *center cockpit.*

and flawlessly fitted clothes. Max, a specialist in the clipped British statement and throw-away line, said, "Doctor Hoyt, here, has done more miles under sail than you have under steam." I mumbled something.

Crusade was sixty-five feet long, cold-molded at Souters, and designed by Alan Gurney. Running in strong winds, she could outsurf *Windward Passage* for distance, if not for speed; reaching, she needed wind to do her very best; to weather, she sailed no better than her rating. The navigator had a separate station beside the midships companionway. There were lockers and drawers for our gear, and a berth opposite the nav-station into the leeward side of which, at alternate changes of watch, I insinuated myself and cameras. I arranged Ray's sea bag at my feet, my sea bag at my chest and shoulders, and put the camera bags between them, about where the soft area of the waist could overlook them. There, on my back, I slept serenely.

We were about in the middle of our class till Lyme Bay, where we went in to escape a foul tide and managed to escape the wind. In the Channel, we watched several boats go by. Going again, we made the

Lizard, where the air came in strong from the south, giving us a roaring reach for the Rock. We passed many of our class and caught the tail-enders in Class I. I got a double-page spread for *Sail* of McCaig in the midships cockpit, the boat throwing bow-wave above the deck on both sides, as we swooped across the Irish Sea under low scud. With no fog, navigation was unexpectedly easy. I was, however, taken aback when I awakened McCaig for his watch and saw that he slept on his side, the small of his back against the cameras. But no remarks were made by my bedfellow, backlog of cameras notwithstanding. Tact is a potent factor in upward mobility.

We finished in the dark, after long surfing runs from the Rock to Plymouth. Our happiest memory was rounding the Rock boat for boat with *Yankee Girl*, high scorer for Cowes Week, and leaving her hull down ninety minutes later. We were surfing every second wave, steam-gauge pinned for ten to twenty seconds at its top of twelve knots. But we eventually took second again, thus setting for me some sort of a record—four successive seconds on *Figaro*, and now, on *Crusade* for her second successive second. We'd lost too much time in Lyme Bay.

Ray McCaig was Commanding Officer, Plymouth, so we left the boat to Max's professional in Milbay Docks, and we went up to Admiralty House where, after a tot and a review of our hopes (since we'd finished rather earlier than most), we slept well.

All the rooms upstairs in Admiralty House were named after famous British admirals: Rodney, Nelson, Codrington, Hood, Saumarez, and so on. I was given "Nelson," which had been furnished with items from Nelson's own sea cabin, including a gimballing bed. In a square box, it was pivoted somehow in line with its longer axis and was stabilized by pins of wood inserted into each side. Nelson's own bed! Nothing could have delighted me more! I reduced myself to under-clothes, pulled the pins, climbed aboard, and gimballed gently till I fell asleep, smiling with delight at an experience greater than three, or anyway the last two Fastnets.

I sent Ray a book of pictures and got a pleasant, hand-written thank you.

A year later, after the Bermuda Race, Kitty and I joined George

Moffett in Edgartown and, after painstakingly adjusting the compass to zero deviation, set out for Greenland on *Snow Goose*, the fourth hull built to the plans (external) of Irving Johnson's final *Yankee*. She was built of steel, and so as she neared the Pole, the increase of magnetic intensity made the correctors incorrect. Whenever the local deviation exceeded thirty degrees, the autopilot went bonkers. On the way, we stopped in Newfoundland, where George had previously cruised and made friends with the sixty-five-year-old Doctor Oliver Green. Wearying of a proper practice in suburban London, Green and his wife had bought a thirty-two-foot Dufour and had sailed to Newfoundland for a greater professional challenge.

We spent several days with them, entertaining one another and being driven by Madam Green hither and thither in search of last minute needs before the Unknown. At some point in the week she made a remark about her "younger brother, the Admiral," whereupon I learned that her maiden name had been McCaig. I was enthusiastic about his courtesy, tolerance, skill, and Nelson's sea bed. She was greatly amused at identifying me. "Oh," she said, Ray has written about you; you're the chap with *all* the cameras!"

I didn't go any further into the matter, but she had a tendency, for the next day or so, to look at me and smile knowingly. In good time we left for Greenland, photographing Bird Island, grounded icebergs, birds everywhere, and a vigorous storm at sea, with *Snow Goose* reaching off at hull speed, rail down, and reefed to the numbers. My bedfellow was my wife, and we had high and low bunks in a double cabin forward of the mast. I had the high bunk with the porthole, but I left the cameras in Kitty's bunk since the bunk was longer than she was and dryer than mine. Once the water temperature gets down toward freezing as of course it does if it's filled with mile-long ice cubes, bronze ports condense the considerable moisture generated by two people breathing; a bathtowel will be filled overnight. Our cabin, which was next to the galley, was very good at condensing and chilly enough at night so that Kitty curled up well clear of the cameras, where I often joined her for warmth.

A year later I got an invitation, rather to my surprise, to the opening cocktail party of a World Global Strategy Conference. I have no notions about global anything, except fewer customs and imigration forms for wandering yachtsmen, but I hastily reviewed my prejudices concerning the same in Antigua, Anguilla, and St. Vincent, and my admiration for the procedures in St. Barts and lack of them in St. Martin. Thus armed, I went off to make my contribution to the conference and exact my tribute from the bar and the hors d'oeuvres.

I presented our engraved invitation at the door of Quarters "A," where the Commanding Officer of the War College elegantly entertains. We were announced to the reception line as "Doctor and Mrs. Hoyt." Third down the line was Ray McCaig, in full admiral kit with ribbons, chicken guts, and that heart-lifting smile of his. "Norry," he said, "my sister wrote you'd sailed north of Newfoundland. You must be mad!," and passed us along. As the party rose to a general roar, he

Snow Goose *off Labrador, New Foundland.*

Snow Goose *in the icebergs—Jakobshafn, Greenland.*

found us in a corner with Mayor Donnelly, Commodore Sayer of the Ida Lewis Yacht Club, and some other Newport types. I made the introductions of "my old shipmate" and turned the floor over to Ray, who brought down the Newport house with a graphic description of trying to get to sleep in a romping sea with four cameras and several lenses attacking the small of his back.

But he loved the pictures, and he had had our two-page spread framed. "It was my first, and probably my last Fastnet," he said, "and a unique experience."

15

Combined Operations

It is one of the truisms of racing that the port watch cannot understand the starboard watch, and that the owner is the last to know. Given executive freedom to get a boat ready for a race, a charge card, and three weeks, I myself have prepared a boat with sufficient creative enthusiasm to be grateful that the owner has retired from summer racing to gainful employment in real life before the toll comes due. On the other hand, when one race follows another, and there's a holdover in Bermuda, even the most carefree owner is likely to outmaneuver ignorance and suggest a brief conference on the bills. And there goes the old game plan.

As a long-time familiar of Newport's shipyards, supervisors, and workers, I had been delegated by Hank duPont to get his new, aluminum, fifty-foot, S&S sloop prepared for the Bermuda Race and the Transatlantic Race to Sweden. The boat was a development of Dr. Giff. Pinchot's yawl, which had won her class in the previous Bermuda Race. Pinchot had described his ideal boat, paid for the tank tests, and S&S had added their magic to the concept and come up with a winner. The basic yawl plan, of course, was Pinchot's.

But it is in the nature of man to try to cap success. As acrobats stand on each others shoulders and go up until the ultimate addition is too much and down they sprawl, so it is with naval architects. To each success with an owner's new concept, they add the expertise of previous successes to carry that development line to its ultimate. Since nothing would convince Rod Stephens that the seven-eighths rig is less than perfect, and nothing would convince Henry B. duPont that anything other than a sloop is a yacht, *Cyane* was a seven-eighths sloop. Unlike Pinchot's *Loki*, *Cyane* went nowhere on her first races. The problem, I was convinced, lay in the sails. I knew, perfectly well, that the hull was great.

There is, however, no greater annihilator of procedure than previous success, and no bond of faith greater than that between a racing owner and a builder of winning sails. Hank had frequent success with Kenny Watts's sails in California, and Kenny had raced with him. Therefore Kenny Watts in California had made the sails for *Cyane* in New England. To suggest they were at fault was equivalent to suggesting the emperor was wearing no clothes. Seeking solutions, I telephoned Olin Stephens and asked him how the sail plan had been designed. "The mast should be exactly parallel with the bulkhead in front of it," he replied. Since there was a three-inch difference between clearance at deck and clearance overhead, I took up on the headstay until the turnbuckle was jammed. There was still a half-inch difference. Stays stretch, particularly headstays, so I got a new one, a foot shorter, and had the old one reswedged six inches shorter, as a spare. The mainsail still didn't set well, so measuring the mast and boom's three point-to-points with a steel tape, sail off, I took the whole main to Thurston, in Warren, and had it recut. The bills went to Wilmington, the day before the Bermuda Race.

We won our class smartly, possibly because we had a good main, possibly because we were in the right places at the right times, possibly because we had a spare working jib after the first blew off its snaps in the gale, and possibly because our mistakes were fewer than the competition's. An ocean race is frequently an exercise in blind luck and comparative ineptitude. In Bermuda, after we had the trophy, I confessed my *lese majesté*. "You recut a Kenny Watts mainsail!" Henry declared, in shock. He ruminated darkly, and then, saving my feelings, he declared, "We need a spare mainsail for the Transatlantic anyway; I'll bet Kenny can make us one and get it here in three days." He could; it didn't look good to me, but we used it. We took third, which cost Hank a Kenny Watts mainsail and dinner for us and the crews and wives of *Figaro* and *Carina*, who'd taken first and second, respectively. A sailmaker at hand is worth two on the phone.

My next attempt at combined operations got even more confused. We were to pick up fifty-foot *Java* at midnight, after we'd been to a party and she had come home from Off Soundings. I'd sail her to Annapolis for Alfred (Rube) Meyer, her owner, to race home; we'd ferry his car from Annapolis. At midnight, all hands met on Burr's Dock, New London, and *Java*'s Off Soundings crew drove off in our car. The Eastern Long Island Sound chart was on the chart table, the engine was still warm, and with Rube Meyer's two sons, my son,

"Hank" du Pont, mid-Atlantic.

daughter, and wife, we took off into the windless, hazy summer night. I had been assured by Rube himself that both tanks had been topped before he left Bristol, Rhode Island, and that he had the full charts from Annapolis to Newport.

The owner is the last to know. Before Rube arrived at Burr's for the Off Soundings Race start, his crew, solemnly saying to themselves,

"This time we'll really give it the old college try!" had lightened the boat by:

1) Pumping 200 gallons of water overboard (the tank held 250).

2) Pumping two 55-gallon drums full of gasoline out (a full tank held 155) and sending it back to the home farm in the pickup.

We ran out of fuel somewhere past New Haven, in the fog, and set the mainsail and the lightest genoa. Early in the afternoon we drifted into Port Jefferson, fueled up, topped off, and motored out. Once again in the Sound, I opened the chart locker for "Western Part" and for charts of New York Harbor. There was nothing there but *Rules of the Road, The Light List,* pencils, erasers, rules, and dividers. The race navigator had saved himself sorting by taking all the charts home, as he later remarked, "to work on."

In my own opinion, there is nothing, *nothing* more absurd than "working on" charts before a race, when you can't possibly know where you're going or how fast you're going till you know the wind speed and direction. And now, having blown ten hours drifting around Long Island Sound, we were deep into our previous schedule for Annapolis. The hell with it—I'd been down Long Island Sound before. We wound up the motor and went along, rounding Execution Rock at about sunset and proceeding, tide with us, under the Throngs Neck and Whitestone Bridges as the light died. By Hellgate, it was dark and getting quite foggy, and by the time we got to Manhattan's East Side, visibility was down to feet. We sounded our way in to the bight by the hospitals and let go the hook. What would the morrow bring?

More fog. The visibility was up to about two hundred yards; enough to get to open water. I got out our only chart while the crew was eating breakfast, made an appropriate latitude-longitude grid on the back of it, and spotted in buoys to get us up the harbor and out past Sandy Hook. Once there we could erase chart one and make chart two. Thank God for the Light List, with its lat-lon for every buoy in the area! Cape May would have charts for the Delaware Bay and the upper Chesapeake.

About where you turn right for Newark, leaving the Narrows, we found some people worse off than we were. Yesterday they'd gone off in a single-engined outboard, no cabin, for fishing off Sandy Hook.

Returning, they'd run into fog and out of fuel. So they tied to one of the buoys on my jackleg chart and waited for succor. By 0930, they were in desperate straits. They were out of cigarettes, and clawing the walls in the depravity of their need. We called the Coast Guard for them, and stood by until they were on their way. But not a soul on *Java* was a smoker. Good-bye victims!

In deference to *Java*'s nine-foot draft, we took the outer channel off Sandy Hook, and bore off down the coast while I erased the New York Harbor grid and set up a New Jersey–Delmarva grid. Shrewsbury Rocks appeared two hundred yards out of the fog, and we set sail in a developing northeast breeze. Fifteen knots was predicted, as well as fog and scattered showers.

And so it went. We passed Barnegat Light in late afternoon, and, in fog, found a buoy off Cape May the next morning by circling in adequate depth in expanding arcs until we found one on my chart. My wife, who specializes in innocent questions designed to open new cans of worms, wondered why I'd plotted all of the Cape May constellation ahead of time, when we could have plotted one after we found it. Rather than acknowledging the justice of her query, I retreated to the chart table for a course and in good time the breakwaters opened their arms to us and we felt our way in, sounding, until we located ten feet of water off a restaurant, and tied there to a schooner masquerading as a buffet-bar. Twenty minutes later we had charts, drinks, and a meal we hadn't cooked. Ole!

By now we were almost a day later than schedule, and we would barely make it before the car arrived with a new lot of bodies for *Java*'s bunks. We rose betimes, and innocently enough, never having been in Cape May before, left in good visibility and light air and took the buoyed, charted channel inside Handkerchief Shoals, Prissy Wick, etc. Never again! Right between a pair of impressively visible buoys, I saw the lazy swells through which we motored bulge, loft, peak, break, and begin again. We headed up outside both buoys to where this wasn't happening, hastily raised sail, strapped genoa and main in, put the wind abeam, and touched shudderingly and lingeringly twice before the swells died and the boat steadied up Delaware Bay. My heart slowly retreated to my chest.

The wind picked up to fifteen over the deck, and we had a great run up Delaware Bay, tide contributing several knots, through the Chesapeake-Delaware Canal, and into the Sassafras River. Without a chart, we found ten to twelve feet up a winding stream I've never since been able to find on a chart. In a perfectly sheltered bend we anchored, at sunset, in a tremendous, sunshine-slashed shower. All hands, in bathing suits, soaped and swam and shouted. The wonderfully soft water made us feel clothed in silk, and the Captain's dinner, the last night out, was steak and french fries and Harvard beets. Within range of target, we went joyously to our bunks.

At noon the next day, we came in to Arnie Gay's dock, to find Rube Meyer there, the car unloaded in a great heap on the end of the dock, and a look of barely restrained impatience on his classic features.

"Where in Hell have you guys been!?!" he queried, straight out of the text from his Green Beret Sensitivity Course. "We've been here two hours!" With great dignity, I refrained from bitter comment. "We're here." I said. "Where's the car?" Of course I did tell the tale in sixty lectures that winter, adding only a little color. Rube sat it out in both the CCA dinner and the Twenty hundred Club dinner. The second time, he even laughed out loud.

Rube is a wonderfully tolerant fellow, and he forgave me my tardiness. In fact, a year or so later, as we were temporarily out of boat, he suggested that we bring his car to him in the Eggemoggin Reach and sail his new boat home. *Aylette* was an Alden Challenger yawl. I'd never seen her specifications. She was as flawless and shiny as a glass eye.

The weather was ideal, and after we took over the boat we went on up to Roque Island. The day we turned around, the fog came down as it can only in Maine and the movies—thick enough to cut and stack. Fogwise, I'm not merely fearless; I've always been lucky. Kitty, on the other tack, is filled with disquiet, nameless apprehensions, and a pervading sense of loneliness. I figure that if you sail a course, check the current on every lobster pot and make small allowances, and go from open buoy to open buoy, at least in North America, you'll probably never have more than an hour's run without a clue. If you know your speed, set the egg timer to go off a minute early, and shut down the engine to listen when powering, you'll make it.

It had never been so foggy. Shores appeared in the Mudhole, Jonesport, Corea, Winter Harbor, Northeast, Blue Hill, Buck, Stonington, and so on, only after we'd anchored and rowed ashore. Behind islands, the wind was light, astern, and almost nonexistent; we motored, Kitty alert as a bird dog on the point. Once anchored, she took on sleep as though stunned. And so it went.

I had no idea how much gasoline Rube's boat used, and not wanting to run out, I put in gallons at every harbor, never topping out. My estimates ranged upward from an initial half gallon an hour to two; probably the propeller was a folding, hemi-demi-semi-sized racing atrocity. More gas!

We filtered into Annisquam, slept, ran the canal, and got twenty-five gallons of gas in Gloucester. Kitty's apprehensions rose to panic at the notion of crossing the traffic lanes into Boston Harbor in thick fog. Fortunately, as we cleared Nahant, the fog lifted to five miles and the northeast breeze zoomed us along. With a sigh of relief, Kitty went to sleep in the cockpit, and the fog closed in again. We found the shore of Scituate Harbor with the dinghy soon after she woke up. I told her the fog had come in again at Minot's Light.

Three days later I delivered the boat to Rube in Bristol. Casually, I asked him how much fuel the tank held. "It's a big one," he said, "a hundred Imperial gallons!" I'd topped it off with a last ten in Newport. Rube went on, "It had about forty in it when you took over. Where the hell have you been?" I didn't mention the fog. I told him how much we'd enjoyed the trip, and we caught the bus to Newport.

The next morning I was dimly awake in my own bed for the first time in weeks when the phone rang. It was 0600. Hank duPont thinks in the night and gets restless by dawn. "Norry," he said, "this is Hank." Resisting the frequent dawn urge to ask, "Hank who?," I murmured, "ummm." "Where have you been?" he asked. "I've been calling for a week." "Sailing," I said. "What I wanted to ask you is: Who's that great sailmaker in Warren?" "Thurston," I said, "Thurston." "Thanks," he said, "I'll be calling you." I yawned before he hung up. "Great," I said.

16

Emergency Overtime Eating

I'VE RACED THREE TIMES transatlantic from Bermuda, and each time experienced problems induced by the fact that the laws and goods in Bermuda have an English rather than an American flavor; for example, what they call "potable water" is a delicate exaggeration. And the circumambient reefs—particularly Black Rock—require daylight, caution, and no advice from people who haven't looked at the chart.

But let's start with the party at George Moffett's. *Guinevere* was racing transatlantic, and George had a new gourmet lady friend who owned two restaurants. She had planned menus-for-eight for twenty four days (she had done quite a bit of cruising), organized the canned goods in appropriate sizes from wholesalers, and ordered four fifteen-pound roasts, some chines of pork, some restaurant rolls of reorganized turkey (packaged so the boneless bicolor slices looked real), lamb chops, and ice cream. Designed by Alan Gurncy with the Troll (she had black, long hair) looking over George's shoulder, *Guinevere* had a great galley, deep freezer, and *équipe* from a cooking boutique. All the canned and packaged food had to be shipped to Bermuda, to be held in bond until twenty-four hours before departure, thus avoiding heavy import duties. The frozen food was to be flown down and picked up from airport to

George Moffett at Guinevere's *helm, Jamaica.*

bond to boat on the last day. But since the steel cans had to be stowed in the aluminum bilge, they had to be magic-marked as to contents, stripped of labels, and given two coats of spar varnish. Thus we hoped to defeat electrolysis and confusion. George and the Troll gave a party in his New York apartment. We rolled up the rugs, laid down newspapers, set up trestles, and gave the cans a final coat. We glowed with anticipation. Such super foods!

But the Bermuda Triangle made its Murphitic influence felt early. On the way down, since George had a new Loran and was curious about it, he fiddled with it one night to see how it worked, and discovered from his shocked navigator that he was forbidden to use it. Actually, the position it gave him checked out with the DR, but he did not tell the navigator anything, because the navigator, Rear Admiral Chick Hayward, exclaimed in horror, "My God, George, we'll have to withdraw from the race! The circular said no electronic equipment for navigation beyond fathometer, RDF, and log." So, though we won our class, George withdrew.

The week in Bermuda was happy. We tied stern-to at Glencoe, ate meals cooked for us, and swam, danced, read, sunned, drank, and made desultory motions toward getting the boat ready for the Transatlantic Race, like storing thirty-six loaves of Pepperidge Farm bread, each loaf baked in a sealed can, in various places in the boat. Bill Rudkin baked it for the fleet, and the technique certainly worked. We stowed the bread so well we didn't find the final loaf till we were cruising in Holland, seven weeks later. It was still fresh, moist, and delicious.

The great day dawned when we had to go to the bonded warehouse to get the shipped food. We lined up with the twenty-odd other skippers, and waited for *Guinevere* to be called. Every one else was called; slowly, fatefully, it dawned on us that we had no varnished cans of food. Our airport crew returned with the frozen items. We called the exporter. "Shucks," he informed us, "it missed the boat, but don't worry, I'll get it on another tomorrow!" Solemnly, we returned to George, a gentle soul who never executed the bearers of bad tidings. Mildly, he inquired, "Has anyone got any good ideas?" Thoughtfully, we stacked the frozen goodies in the deep freezer.

Alan Gurney and I went immediately to Teddie Gosling's supermarket, I because I'd helped supply boats for several Transatlantic

Races and Alan because he knew English food, which has names like Bonkers, Wheatabix, and Gentlemen's Relish. Teddie wasn't exactly ecstatic about turning us loose in his store while he went home for the night, but desperation lends conviction to discussion, and we set to it.

The idea was that we'd work up a day's menu, stack it on the floor, and package it against the bilge. Teddie had an ice machine out in front, with a bag dispenser, and we had an Allen wrench. We took the machine apart, packaged the menus in ice bags, and twenty-four bags later, drove over to Glencoe and stowed the food in the bilge. We felt we had defeated the Bermuda Triangle, and we slept the sleep of the slightly apprehensive. Predicted weather for the start was force six to seven, southwest.

At dawn the worst was plain—it was blowing like stink and raining. We bravely started the motor, pulled down a reef, and motored around Hamilton and out off St. George, where the committee boat was rolling gunwale to gunwale. We cut the engine, hoisted the working jib, the main, and the jigger, and started to race to Copenhagen. That evening, reeling and bouncing through developing seas, we locked the shaft and started the engine for generating. But it didn't start. The starter had locked on earlier, and burned out. We had no electricity, no deep freezer, and only what radio and lights the current batteries could supply. The boat was new, and it had none of what I now regard as compulsory spares: a spare starter, a spare alternator, a spare raw-water pump, a spare fresh-water pump, spare injectors, a spare fuel pump, spare belts, a set of gaskets, an assortment of hoses, a fiberglass kit, plugs, hose clamps, an American flag of suitable size, and a prayer book.

Meanwhile, we went on Emergency Overtime Eating. The ice cream was served all around almost at once—big helpings in the cold and rainy cockpit and below decks. We started cooking, turkey first. After turkey dinner, turkey sandwiches, and turkey hash, we threw about twenty pounds of turkey roll overboard. The white meat had puce overtones, and nobody was hot for turkey. Roast beef next; I cut the second roast into cubes, made *carbonnade de boeuf flamande,* and poured in half a bottle of red wine while it simmered. Cooled, I stored

OVERLEAF: *"It was blowing like stink."*

it in a Tupperware jug and sunk it in the coldest section of the bilge. As the top layer of the deep freezer gradually melted, we ate our way through pork, lamb chops, the last of the ice cream, and the third roast beef. Cabot Lyman, a guileless youth at the time, was supervising the cooking, and when I asked him to pour off a little of the fat to be reserved for the second round of Yorkshire pudding, he opened the gimballed stove incautiously. Once off balance, it ejected the roast, which caromed around the boxlike cooking area, spewing fat, while Cabot tried to block it into a corner with his right Topsider.

It was a sight to be long remembered. Four members of the crew slept, their bellies wandering across their stomach muscles as the ship swooped and heeled, blissfully unaware of Cabot's frantic pursuit in their midst. We got the roast re-ovened; we made two pans of Yorkshire pudding; all fifteen pounds of the roast vanished in a meal. At the end of ten days we were through all the raw meat fit to eat, and we went onto the canned menus. Meanwhile, carrying main and mizzen spinnakers, and driving hard in fresh winds, we'd worked out a lead and were happy.

The rest of the race was uneventful except for the night of the big bang. It sounded off about 0200 of a moonless night as we were running hard under reefed main and spinnaker. After the bang, nothing unusual transpired, so we pressed on, regardless, into the noisy night. Dawn revealed the spinnaker halyard block nesting on top of the spinnaker, and the wire halyard two feet down a slot it had sawed in the mast. Tony, our professional, went up the mast to fix it. Thereafter we carried the bag on two halyards, and we went aloft daily to renew shackles as needed. If things are bound to wear, the crew should make the decision, not the things; so we used bronze screw shackles on stainless hangers and stainless clevises.

We won our class. Pat Haggerty's *Bay Bea* towed us in. The instant he was cleared by customs and immigration, Cabot dove into Copenhagen harbor and swam ashore to Heidi, thus capturing her heart and later marrying her. The stew in the bilge, with a bit more red wine, had been palatable fifteen days after it was cooked, and the good stuff from Teddie Gosling's had served us well, as we drifted motorless, through the calms in the Kattegat. Everyone on board gained weight on the trip.

The next winter, George took second to *Figaro* in the SORC, sold the boat, and began building a traditional, gaff-rigged, three-jibbed sloop.

Two years after the Copenhagen Race, I started again on a Bermuda-Transatlantic coupling, this time on Thor Ramsing's *Solution*. I knew the Triangle was lying in wait. And it got us, twice. First, it came on a gale with Bermuda a day away. We smashed along, rail down, and being driven toward the several miles of shallows on the northwest side of the "still vexed Bermoothes." As navigator, I was apprehensive—loran forbidden, Bermuda's two RDFs relocated together so they denied cross-bearings, and the bottom rising instantly from infinity to fifteen fathoms, and thence to inadequate depths. The fathometer was erratic, what with ten-foot waves lofting us around, and the angle of heel varying from twenty to forty-five degrees.

Wave shapes are pretty standard—offshore they are cyclic, and then, as the bottom comes up, epicyclic—which is to say that the crested tops, offshore, are frothy and soft, but as land affects them, the crests rise from the depths of the wave at about fifty degrees, with the front face long and sloping. Coming from the deeps, you hit the epicyclic waves, drive up the long slope, and rocket off the top into a ten-foot void. Under such circumstances, it is advisable to ease around the crest rather than leave it by air.

So, the inevitable happened. Charlie X, a college student with large muscles and superb coordination, our best foredeck man, was in the head on the windward side of the boat, his boots on, his rain gear around his ankles, together with his pants and underpants, when we ejected from a wave crest and fell ten feet, sideways, onto the rocklike rising slope of the next wave. The head had a sliding door, high against which Charlie's feet were braced. His weight, the impact of fourteen tons of boat stopping in midfall, and the thinness of the panels were fatal—his feet broke through the panel, he slid off the seat with his knees cocked over his head, and effectively trapped himself. At this point, the fathometer went abruptly from mindless blankness to fifteen fathoms. I shouted "Tack! Tack!" We tacked, and poor Charlie was hanging from his heels. For most of us, the situation had humor.

We finished later, sometime after 0200, in the rain. I left the deck to record our time and get a course for the channel to Hamilton.

Meanwhile Charlie, extricated from his dilemma but probably suffering from judgmental inversion, urged Thor to "Go in there; those lights must be the committee boat!" Thor, having been awake for two days and nights, went in there, across Black Rock. There was a mighty banging bounce, we swung back out, aware of error, and I surged on deck with appropriate remarks for people who gave navigational advice without looking at a chart.

Thor Ramsing

But really it was the Bermuda Triangle. It had gotten to Charlie earlier. Fortunately, it never got to the food, which arrived complete. And it never got to the deep freezer, which lasted to Spain. We crossed without any emergency overtime eating.

17

The Perfectionist

ERIK'S FATHER had been an atomic physicist and distinguished in his field, his mother a brilliant woman with a powerful will. Erik, at twenty-five years of age was an honors graduate from experimental Bard College, a candidate for the Ph.D., and a teaching assistant at Brown University. An excellent instructor, he taught his own meticulously prepared courses. But he lived for and dreamed boats. Like baseball and football nuts, he could give you the lineage and statistics of almost any boat in the harbor, of any naval architect's training, and of most builders' output. He and I once played a game with vintage yachts in the Virgin Islands, studying the lines and the rig, and then assigning them to Billy Atkin, Paine, Warner, or Burgess. Erik even recognized such British designers as Robb, Illingworth, Nicholson, and Giles.

As a youth, he had accompanied his terminally ill mother to Anguilla. There he helped build a shore cottage and then embarked as ship's boy on the venerable trading schooner *Warspite* down island and back. He eventually inherited from his father a Tartan 28, which he immediately had hauled out and set about perfecting. He rubbed the hull eelslick with 800 wet-or-dry, wet. He Awl-gripped it to a mirror gloss, and stripped and varnished the token teak trim with six coats. He polished cleats, stanchions, and pulpits; he installed multicolored cordage. He scrubbed, sanded, and Awl-gripped the bilges! He then sailed the boat for two weekends and sold it to a hungry buyer. He had a strange, wild look as he told me about it.

"Erik," I said, "have you lost your mind? You spent half the

summer getting that boat in flawless condition and then sold it?" He
reached behind him, looking stranger still. He unrolled dog-eared blueprints. "I've bought another boat," he glowed. "It's a classic Wink
Warner forty-two footer, built by Luke, *and the surveyor had only two*
pages of recommendations! The sails are two years old and have hardly
been used. She's named *Snapper.*" "How old is she?" I asked. "She was
built in 1936," he admitted. "Original engine and rig?" I asked. "Well
. . . ," he admitted, "I enjoy working on boats." I resisted the impulse
to be Old Mother Hoyt and ask him "What *HAVE* you *DONE?*"

He soon found out. Over the next two years as the boat sat in
Johanssen's yard, Erik ran up bills and worked them out with Johanssen
on other boats. He bought a new engine at a "great bargain," a new
head to replace the verdigrised "classic," took out the entire cabinetry,
discovered cracked ribs and laminated in new, replaced the horn timber, took all woodwork down to the wood and refinished her, inside and
out, stripped and bleached and reconditioned the teak decks and teak-
decked trunk cabin, renewed the lifelines, replaced the cracked swedge
fittings with Norseman fittings and toggles. A few planks displeased
him, so out they came, and he learned how to replace them perfectly.
By the time you could no longer see inside from outside, he had
modified the layout, undercoated the hull planking so elegantly he
could have varnished the whole boat. He discovered, in the archives of
its manufacturer, a no-longer-produced sextagonal binnacle in brass and
glass. To replace the browned, flat compass, he found a spherical; he
regalvanized the Herreshoff anchor and bought a Bruce. After much
internal and external debate, he bought thirty feet of stainless chain for
the anchor (at six dollars a foot!).

For Erik, I was the gray eminence, being thirty plus years older, a
veteran of some five boats, twenty-three transatlantics, and the cruising
of most coasts of the United States and Europe. On the other hand,
I had not reconditioned anything completely, although I had built a
Dolphin from a raw hull and deck. My yachting philosophy stemmed
from prolonged membership in the O.P.B.C., with its years of racing
and cruising in Other People's Boats. Serious ocean racers are commit-
ted to frequent new boats, spectacular annual expenditures, and premature discoveries of everything that can go wrong with boats and what

to do about it. I had owned boats because (1) I felt naked without one, (2) I loved cruising with my wife and children, and (3) a nearly new boat that needed reasonable re-styling by me could be sold for a profit.

In our wooden boat years, I had been somewhat in the same situation as Erik. I had done my own maintenance, sanding metallic paint off bottoms and filling my hair, armpits, and mouth with a two-day increment of copper. I'd sanded and painted topsides, and even completely burned off (without scorching) *Wagtail*'s cedar-planked hull, despite the doom-saying of the yard's professionals. After having given it a painstaking undercoat and two coats, nicely sanded, of International French Gray, I had stepped back to admire the flawless gloss of the final coat. Finding myself in midair (I'd been painting on a trestled plank), I discarded the remaining paint, which caught up with me after I landed, thus verifying the yard workers' predictions, but shifting the disaster category.

I'd developed enough painting skill, after the first boat, to excite the approval and cupidity of Frank Norton, who owned our small shipyard in Newport. He permitted me to do my own work providing I'd work for him on demand at half the normal wages. After all, I was a schoolteacher and worked for half-pay anyway.

Though Frank was a good friend, he had a spectacularly low boiling point which I feared to excite. Occasionally, however, it worked to my advantage; for instance, on the day when U.S. naval launches were preventing stepping the mast on my *Wagtail*. Despite harbor regulations, they were operating at only two speeds: full ahead and full reverse. Being designed to carry crowds rather than to go through water, the launches were spreading prodigious wakes, in which *Wagtail* was rolling and pitching. Norton telephoned the naval base, and got a tactless, green ensign, who told him, "If you'll identify the vessels, we'll do our best to slow them down." Frank asked him to hold the line, took a rifle from the corner of the shop, and shot holes in the bows of the next three launches to pass the dock. "I've identified three launches by shooting holes in their bows," he announced over the phone. "How many more do you want me to identify?" And for the next hour, they crept and we stepped.

Frank's economic sense educated me. "You can't afford romance," he said. "You've got $10,000 in this boat, and a hundred hours a year work. If $10,000 don't bring in $1,000 a year, your boat's just romance. Lemme find you charters—you race anyway half the summer." He found me a month's worth, two weeks at the beginning of the summer (Off Soundings, and the Bermuda or Annapolis Races) and two weeks at the end (Vineyard and Off Soundings Races). The charters, since they hoped to meet Frank's approval, were perfect. They brought the boat back as spotless as a new refrigerator. Frank had told them, "Pay when you get back, and buy anything she needs." Thanks to Frank, I made an annual profit on three over-equipped boats in a row, selling them at prices that increased at a better pace than inflation, probably because they got great exposure.

So Erik's feckless infatuation with romantic perfection excited my supervisor syndrome. Echoing Frank, I pointed out that Erik had at least $40,000 in *Snapper* (he'd been totally secretive about what he'd paid or still owed). The year was 1982, and even the money market was paying 10 percent, insurance was costing him $1,200, and he was making himself feel economical by locating wholesale outlets for the very best paint, varnish, brushes, tools, and all the other supplementary items a boat demands. At the very best, *Snapper*'s ownership was making a $15,000 difference a year in Erik's basic funding, probably more. Meanwhile, for two more years, *Snapper* built up yard bills, and Erik painted, varnished, and did better woodwork inside than Chippendale, Hepplewhite, and Sheraton in concert. About fortnightly, romance faded to common sense, and he drove down to Newport and us in his rust-laced 1972 Pontiac wagon. Discussion made him feel better. While I was free to point out that nothing I said had *yet* resulted in rectifying decisions, he explained that knowing "exactly where he stood" was important to him.

At Brown, he was now down to taking one course, teaching two, and teaching on the side at a junior college to support his habit. That fall, Kitty and I intermittently drove to the boatyard, where Erik led us through the new wonders as he scraped the 3M off the perfected decks, wet-or-dried the perfected rails for another coat, or revealed the splendid new bronze deck winch that he'd "found." She was to be launched in the spring of 1983, so he could take day charterers sailing during the America's Cup trials and finals.

In March, Erik showed up, delighted with himself—he'd passed his Coast Guard exams to skipper—sail and steam up to X-teen tons coastwise—and was embarked on studies for the next step. In June he stopped by again. He'd found a stainless vane gear in like-new condition, was improving it slightly with a few stainless weldments, and had taken out *Snapper's* bowsprit and Samson posts to splice in some dutchmen at the base, where the oak was black and may have "begun to go." *Snapper* spent another summer in the yard, had her mast scraped raw and thoroughly sanded and varnished. She was launched in the fall for the Wooden Boat Show, where she was vastly admired. When the twelve-meter *Gleam* won the *Concours d'élégance*, what with it being an America's Cup year, Erik did not quite cry.

During the summer, Erik's uncle had died and left a pretty fat egg in Erik's nest. His disappointment at not winning was alleviated characteristically. He bought *Sockeye,* a thirty-eight foot Augie Nielsen aluminum sloop, also built by Paul Luke, and splendidly equipped with sails, electronics, and all International Offshore Rule (IOR) requirements for offshore races. I figured, by Frank Norton's standards, that Erik had now diminished his putative income by at least $30,000 a year.

He and I had not discussed this purchase at all. He even introduced his new mistress in a sneaky way, showing me the blueprints, asking me what I thought of *Sockeye,* going over the listed equipment, the suggested price ($70,000), and asking me if I thought she'd "go" for $60,000. I said the price seemed to me very reasonable, and the boat wasn't so extremely IOR as to require an excessive crew, or to be uncruisable and unsalable. Then he confessed to having purchased her at "well below the listing."

"Erik," I said, "has she complete double-wiring for her electrical panel?" She had. I remembered how Huey Long used to switch from one set of circuits to another in the first aluminum *Ondine* to see which setup generated the least electrolysis on that particular day. I remembered how Paul Wolter took all the teak trim off Tom Watson's aluminum *Palawan* and bedded it in thick 3M, to keep the metal from bubbling as salt water formed acid from the wood. I remembered how the aluminum bell on my roller furling gear completely eroded away the bronze bevel gear bolted to it, causing the gear to disintegrate in the middle of the Gulf Stream.

"Erik," I said, "aluminum?!?"

He was ready for me. "Norry, you remember you figured that $15,000 was break-even in income for *Snapper?*" I did. "I've had an offer for her for next summer—a full summer charter to one man, with his own skipper, for $15,000, with an option to buy."

"Grab it!," I said. "But what are you going to do with this one?" He thought he'd crew her on short charters while he restyled her a little, made her more luxurious and comfortable—yachted her up. He itched to show her off. Would we join him on *Snapper* for a weekend cruise to Stonington, where *Sockeye* was berthed?

We had no time, as we would be leaving for Oregon in two days. But Erik found two of our friends with whom, as guest, he had frequently cruised, and they were delighted. Like me, they had worried over Erik's unresolved conflict between being a nautical entrepreneur and a college professor. Now with two rental properties, he could make restoring a hobby, generate income summers, and gradually wean himself from wood, aluminum, and attendant complexity. At last he could work toward scholarly repute and fulfillment. In exudations of euphoria, the expedition wheeled Erik's new inflatable toward the waterfront on Erik's new collapsible, bicycle-wheeled dolly. "Fair laughed the morn, and soft the zephyr smiled . . ."

Our plane was leaving Boston at 1800, Monday. Late Sunday afternoon, Erik arrived with his guests to leave his inflatable in our back yard. He was in the rancid, unreasonable temper of a farrowing sow, and directed my attempts to help with heated impatience, recalling Schiller's "Mit der Dummheit kämpfen Götter selbst vergebens."* Monosyllabically, he saw his guests off. They were filled with admiration for the new acquisition, having prowled it in wonder.

Erik came inside and sat down with the élan of a bag of shot. "God!" he said, "I'll never be able to take out charter parties!" Erik had been our guest (and useful helper) in Costa Rica, the Virgins, and Maine. "It's a lot easier to be a guest than to be a skipper," I remarked,

*Stupidity makes the Gods themselves despair.

thus praising myself. He exploded, "They got cigarette ashes everywhere, and he tapped out his pipe on my varnished rail without even thinking!" He simmered a while. "Everything got left everywhere while I was busy sailing." Finally, in an almost reasonable tone, he said, "and they had three drinks while I got dinner, and then weren't very hungry." "Why didn't you ask her to get dinner?" I asked. *"In my galley?,"* he snarled.

Plainly, Erik's standards disqualified him as a charter skipper. We abandoned his problem and headed for Oregon. But waiting around in Denver for the second leg of our trip, I foresaw *Sockeye* three years in the boatyard, and Erik stripping and bedding trim, sanding undercoating, and Awlgripping, Interthaning, or Durathaning the hull, doing a Ph.D. thesis on electrolysis, redesigning the galley, and studying fabrics and color theory to amplify visual space. In a way, you have to admire someone who can go totally with his inner compulsions.

We flew home in October, and Erik met us at the airport. During the summer he'd rented the downstairs apartment in our Newport house, and was eager to see us—to show and tell. Erikly, he meticulously contained obvious pressure, fended off our questions about *Snapper* and the new boat, evinced fascination with my enthusiasm for Northwest cruising, and finally, as Dorchester passed on the left, casually opened his wallet and passed me a calling card.

"Erik!," I whooped, "what's this?"

THE PERFECTIONIST

Boats prepared for sale or for you

*"A meticulous standard gets a
Meticulous Price"*

ERIK SKARSTROM

29 Pope Street
Newport, R.I.

401-847-0310

"I've sold *Snapper*, *Sockeye*'s chartered out at $20,000, and I have two boats to work up. Y'know, I've got people doing some of the work, Johanssen gives me a percentage on the billings, and . . ." His voice faded out, and he accelerated past a roaring trailer truck. We approached the Route 24 turnoff.

What was that?," I asked. "I couldn't hear you."

"I've bought another boat," he said.

18

My Days with
Bob Baker

I was sitting in the headmaster's office, for no good reason other than Headmaster Willet L. Eccles liked to stop work and reminisce, when Bob Baker presented himself, looking for a job. He was tall, lean, indifferent to salary (Eccles eyes lighted up—St. George's was running over budget and under enrollment objectives), but he wanted to be housed and fed. He did not (repeat *not*) have any desire to be a housemaster or to be directly involved in the management or discipline of boys. He wanted to run the shop.

For many years, the shop had been run by Ray Fritz, an arbitrary, talented methodical man of German extraction. The shop had been divided into separate areas, and every boy began his career as a woodworker by making a pen tray out of mahogany, hand carved (even though pens were on the way out), and sanded and sanded and varnished and varnished and hand rubbed with rottenstone and oil. Finished, it showed how well wood could be finished, and how thoroughly boys (some of them) could be bored, and how much time could be spent in the outer precincts of the shop in your virgin year. In the inner precincts, you weren't allowed to stand behind a saw, you had to make your own push-stick with a handsaw. There were ten wood-turning lathes in the next section for the third exercise on the Fritz schedule —turning a bowl, (and sanding a bowl and varnishing a bowl, and hand rubbing a bowl).

But we're off the Baker Trail. In the week before Bob showed up,

Ray Fritz had escalated his areas of disagreement with the headmaster to the extent that steam fogged the windows when the two passed each other. In real life, Fritz was a successful contractor, a member of a winning barbershop quartet, and a member of the national championship rifle team. He felt that his random afternoons on the campus were in the nature of a favor that the school should damn well be grateful for, however he ran his show, ordered his materials, and kept the books on his operation. He had therefore left, taking some of the machinery with him (not that he really wanted it) to frustrate Willet.

Eccles saw in Bob an artless artist, a controllable subject, a willing subordinate. Little did he know. Deep in the Baker blood there ran a strain of stubborn opposition to the status quo, a will to reshape the world to his heart's desire (beautiful in shape and leisured in time, preferably cast in the eighteenth century when gaff rig, boots, and pipe smoking were enough to let a man function). He was hired. I had the freedom of the shop as part of my contract. Fritz had found me a bit of a thorn, as I'd learned in our family woodworking factory and was more production minded and less finicky than either Baker or Fritz. But Bob and I took joy in our first joint enterprise, tearing out the partitions, removing the electric buzzer releases on the intersection doors, and removing the aligned assortments of lathes, benches, desks, etc. Bob traded in half the lathes for a good band saw, managed somehow to get a thickness planer by joining forces and letting the maintenance men into the shop (Fritz had foamed when they came near the door, as one of them once had borrowed a tool and left it on the bench, not on its colored silhouette on the wall), and then embarked on a career of boatbuilding.

I had a boat in the harbor; it was made of wood and double-ended. It met Bob's approval, and it needed a dinghy because I had children and when we were cruising the one dinghy we had was rarely available to adults. I wanted a pram.

First we had several days of discussions. I had a sailboat, so I didn't need a sailing pram, just a pram. Negative. It wasn't the first time my mind was to be made up for me. But we had a wonderful time. First we experimentally bent marine plywood till it began to fray splinters along the bend. Then we relaxed it about five degrees and accepted that arc as the bow sweep. The size was decided because a sheet of plywood is eight feet long, and two sheets would make the boat, sides and bottom, and seats. The building form gave us a serendipity—the bow went a little hollow, and the hollow was compensated for by the rounding of the stern. Bob leapt on the plywood's willingness and made the stern rounder to add to the bow flare.

The little Puddleduck sailed like a champion, and we took one to a dinghy regatta on a lake in Massachusetts, where we wiped out our class so thoroughly that we were moved up one class, where we took second. Drinking a certain amount of beer in celebration, we made our uncertain way to a friend's house (no notice to him, of course) and a nightful of smiling sleep.

The little boats took the imagination of two parents, and we proposed to reinstitute St. George's sailing program our own way. I got donations of fastenings from George Stone's Independent Nail and Packing, of sailcloth from Bainbridge. We charged the kids $50 for a boat, sailaway, the labor theirs. But we found that kids run out of gas unless they are keeping up with the crowd, and gradually, the open spaces where the lathes had once been were occupied with half-finished, and quarter-finished dinghies that the kids weren't getting on with, while the more skilled, more diligent, or more careless were out sailing. So we moved in an icebox, screwed a hasp on it, put in beer, and locked it against the young. And after the little beggars were in bed, Baker, Jim Keegan, Redwood Wright, Charlie Knowles, Dave Pratt, and a raft of others of lesser leisure joined us to put in screws, putty joints, slap on paint, fit seats, sand centerboards, and drink beer. Miraculously, a fleet of Puddleducks made it to the school beach.

Baker's instructional techniques were only a touch better than the sink-or-swim variety. We'd shove the kids out in the dinghies, with their pretty shaped rudders in one tiller hand and their elegant sails in the other (sliding gunter rig, of course), with the southwest wind blowing them and sand off the beach. Some would find out what to do at once, a few would drift farther out, cast loose the sheet, paddle with the rudder, and earnestly request advice.

Baker would sail out, pipe in jaw, lank frame elegantly draped all over the little boat, and nudge alongside the victim, suggesting as he

herded the helpless child that he pull in the sheet, pull the tiller toward him, let out the sheet a little, and center the tiller. As the sail took the wind and the boat reached in toward the shore, Baker would slide away smiling complacently—*quod erat demonstrandum.*

The shop went in much the same way. Lumber began to pile up in corners. Bills accumulated in the little room plastered to the side of the building where Baker's office was—you could see east, west, and north from there, and it wasn't heated in winter (which, mainly skin and bone as he was, he must have minded, but he loved the snug privacy of it). The kids were involved with projects as grandiose as they could muster or as simple as they liked, and as gloriously disorganized as nature itself. There was a faint feeling among the young that Baker's grasp on sanity was marginal, at best, but they managed to manage him into helping with some of their problems, and they worked out the rest themselves. I don't think he ever gave anyone unnecessary advice, and he certainly gave as little advice as he could. Partly, I think, he couldn't believe that they couldn't see as clear a line as he could.

Meanwhile, in his little cube of a room, he was drawing boats, making delicious small models, smoking his pipe, and disapproving of the straight sheers and scamped underbodies of the latest development of the Sparkman and Stephens line. I took Olin Stephens over to Bob's cubicle once, and prowled with him through Bob's drawings. Olin pensively and nostalgically summarized the drawings with, "I've never been able to do a character boat." They lived in different countries.

Bob was also pretty cute. In the past, he'd had the hots for one of the Ashley* girls, who were real objects of desire with elegant voices, wads of serenity, and figures that would make you bite the sheet. As a delicate gesture of his regard, he presented one of them with a model of an eighteenth-century sloop, about two-and-a-half inches long and remarkably detailed. It was fixed to its builders blocks, also detailed, and the whole sat on top of a wee chest, tapered to the top and dovetailed at the corners. The lid could be turned over so that the boat could be stored, safe from harm, in the chest. But like non-craftsmen in general,

*The *Ashley Book of Knots* Ashleys!

Baker in one of the boats he built.

the Ashley goddess had less control of her fingers than of Bob, and her handling hadn't helped the model, which she returned to him, full of confidence in her octane rating, for repair. Perfidy he could accept; clumsiness, never. He repaired the model and kept it as a souvenir of illusion.

Bob loved junk. I was coaching crew at the time, and Bob did a lot of repairing on the shells, which, older than our competition's stuff, needed constant refurbishing. Ray Fritz used to fix the metal stuff in his home workshop, as we were still on terms of mutual respect and subcutaneous amusement at each other's character traits; Bob would do the woodwork.

Bob was a sucker to go on any expedition, anywhere. So when Yale was breaking up and selling its harbor boathouse, I got Bob to run down there with me to see if we could pick up an ancient eight or two for our young and, just perhaps, a single or two for me. I got two wherrys for $100, and two eights, black with aggravated, cracked varnish, free for the school, and twenty oars, also veterans.

While I was improving each dusty hour in the boat house, Bob prowled, and came to me with his eyes aglow. He'd found an antique coaching launch, and it was available for giving away. It was four feet wide, twenty-three feet long, and had a big, slow-turning engine that dated back to the administration of Rutherford B. Hayes; the stem was held together with a great brass weldment narrow as a butcher's blade, and the mahogany planking had suffered several years of drying out so that the seams were transpicuous. The fuel tanks, saddled on either side of the after end, were copper and beautifully patinaed. The outboard rudder was strung to the wheel with ancient linen lines, which degenerated into dust at the touch. It belonged in a Hollywood movie about a deserted house. So we accepted it.

Yale agreed to set it afloat and restring the rudder. They were so grateful that we wanted it and that Baker loved it that they even had the engine running. They furnished us with a giant, galvanized iron, old-fashioned pump, a pipe with a wooden stick in it, a flapper at the bottom, and a leather conical cup attached to the wooden stick that pulled water up the pipe and emitted it in long slurps out a side spout. The boat's seams had been filled with soft soap, and it had had a week to swell in the waters of the harbor. It floated. The engine started. We left in the light of dawn before any wind got up and throbbed toward Newport at about fifteen knots, the giant propeller beneath us thrusting us along with visible pulses, like a great beating heart.

The ocean was mirror flat past the Thimbles, past Duck Island Roads, past New London, and through Fisher's Island Sound. But from Watch Hill to Point Judith the swells were running, and it was quite lumpy off Judy. By the time we rounded it was afternoon, and we were in a modest southwester, only having to pump three-quarters of the time. I caught the rhythm of the engine, and the general effect as seen by Mrs. J. N. Brown from *Bolero* as it passed us, and I paused, waved, and went back to the task, which was that each gout of the pump urged the boat exactly the distance of the spurt. Baker sat on the fire-engine bench behind the wheel, forward, throbbing with delight, steering with delicate fingers caressing the mahogany wheel, at ease in Zion.

Fortunately, the launch tore loose from its mooring off Third Beach (the stem pulled out) and sank after my happy spring of coaching crew from it, and Baker didn't have to spend his miniscule salary and his summer vacation restoring it to give it away. Instead, his summer was occupied by the Block Island Cowhorn, which is now in the Mystic Museum.

Baker had borrowed one of the school's boats, and with Pratt, Keegan, Knowles, and Wright, the lot of them had gone to Block Island for a merry weekend. Baker had had several beers, grown bored and miffed at something, and wandered the fields and uplands coping with his misanthropy, which came and went with the weather. He found an abandoned cowhorn, returned and became a happy part of the party, unable to rest till he got back to school and conned me into sailing out to Block Island and towing this orphan of the storm home. By this time it was fall, and we were back from cruising. Bob had found a little money, and he had the boat in decent shape for towing.

Back in Newport with the cowhorn, we gave the seized-up brass and cast-iron engine away in a characteristic episode: I took my dinghy, and we tied the cowhorn astern, to be rowed from Norton's Shipyard at the north end of Newport Harbor to Williams and Manchester's at the south end of the harbor. With a big propeller and engine, the cowhorn towed like a boat tied to the shore with a rubber band. It would go exactly as far as I stroked, stop, and go again. Baker sat aft, negligent hand on the tiller, a look of ineffable content on his face. He was admiring her lines. The very feel of the original builder was at the center of his sensations. At Wms and M., the stern was lifted by a crane, the propeller was taken off, the engine was unbolted and taken out for rebuilding as an historical example of the famous Mianus make-and-break, brass pipes, petcock, and all. A plug was put in the shaft hole, and we were re-lowered into the water so that I could row it back to Norton's. (Norton was another of the people who admired Bob's great talent for design, woodwork, and falling in love with elegant shapes.)

The cowhorn slid along as you wouldn't believe. I had to row double time to keep it from overrunning me. From his indolent ease, Bob kept exclaiming on how sweetly she ran, how beautiful the hull form was, how elegantly the swing of the wood and the tensions of the frames balanced out. Two years of his spare time later, he gave it away looking as crisp as new.

For all his love of boats, he darkly distrusted stuff like spinnakers, bloopers, and the manifestations of the racing instinct. We were bringing home one of the school's larger boats one beautiful late spring night; there was moonlight and a fifteen-knot steady southwest wind. I went up at 2000 to relieve Bob's watch, set the spinnaker, and have a lovely sail up the long beach from Watch Hill. Midnight came, and Bob's watch slept. It *was* a lovely night, so we jibed at Point Judith, sailed all the way to Newport without calling him out, anchored and slept. In the morning he grumped at us. "I suppose you guys carried that damn thing all night?" If its vintage wasn't Hornblower's, Baker couldn't approve.

Along about this time Red Wright's sister, Anna, appeared on the scene, and Baker abandoned a demi-courtship of Becky Buell, in whose company he gazed at landscape, admired architecture, and smoked his pipe meditatively. Bob and Anna were as bad a match as one could imagine, passion aside. Anna was as positive as thunder and lightning, ruthlessly argumentative in defense of her systematically liberal opinions. (She had been a very strong member of a Communist cell at

Pembroke and was rewarded with a trip to Russia, where, her baggage searched daily, she became an equally ardent anti-Communist and worked for young Herbert Hoover's commission, which later exposed that prominent Philadelphian theorist, Alger Hiss.) Redwood and I did our best to prevent the union, but of course we underestimated the basic contrariness of both parties and probably added a bit of determination to what was already a mutual bonfire.

Married, Baker spent more and more time away from home to avoid discussions he didn't need about subjects that didn't move him to passion. He took weekends in Westport with his old buddies, whose picture of our Robert was not mine (or Anna's). There he worked desultorily on a series of small boats, pretty skiffs, and two commissioned restorations—a catboat and, if I remember rightly, some Whitehall skiffs he discovered under the porch of a half-abandoned summer hotel in California. I guess it was at this point that Anna's energy took on the Great Puddleduck Campaign.

Boat shows were just becoming a thing, and the Bakers set up a production line of Puddleducks at about $250 each, sailaway, which was financed, directed, and extensively implemented by Anna. Bob, confused by the faint embers of ambition, the bellows of flattery, and the smoke screen of resentment at being organized, advertised, and relentlessly employed, almost immediately found two splendid outlets for the fires of frustration. He bought a ladder fire engine to carry the Puddleducks hither and thither. It was splendidly painted a good rich red, with gold stripes, and it had siren, spotlight, and brass handholds. The department locale was taken off the fire-engine door and regilded with the Puddleduck logo. His second maneuver, with Anna's compliance, was to get her pregnant and thus refocus her energy. The Puddleduck venture died a natural death after two children and a divorce, the Moby Dick pulpit venture,* and Anna's inheritance of the whole responsibility for building, marketing, and collecting.

By this time, Bob was getting the occasional commission to design and build, and had abandoned St. George's. He and Headmaster Eccles got along famously, Eccles approving Bob's general air of secret wisdom

---

*Bob built Father Mapple's pulpit for the New Bedford church to which Melville had assigned it. He lost money at the job, but it's beautiful.

and the effect of letting the kids educate themselves and thus acquire
critical acumen and self-confidence. But Bill Buell succeeded Eccles as
headmaster, and had a policy of prowling the purlieus, piously urging
organization, order, and neatness. By this time, the shop had been
thoroughly invaded by Bud Worthley's boys; his maintenance crew had
filled the benches with their junk, and they had made one end of the
shop into a garage. This situation generated a position of mutual irre-
sponsibility for the overall appearance, and the problem was generally
solved by keeping the garage door shut.

Along about this time, Bob and I got involved in designing the
Gosling. I'd chartered our *Wagtail* (a thirty-two-foot Rhodes double-
ended cutter, planked in cedar and finished inside with raised face
panels of waxed butternut) to some friends for a late season cruise, and
they had been threatened by a modest hurricane in Cuttyhunk. Setting
both anchors on chain and tying the dinghy astern, they had flown out
of the threatened area. The boat survived the hurricane with no dam-
age other than a shredded flag (they had been in a hurry), but the
dinghy, a big Oldtown with a solid mahogany transom and bent cedar,
canvas-covered hull, was located full of water at the foot of the harbor.
We went there and, lo, only the upper foot of it still existed. The
bottom had abraded away on the stony shore. It was insured.

Bob was filled with enthusiasm. "We'll design a sailing dink that
will beat everything and look like a boat, not a box," he enthused, and
he showed up a week later with lines, a table of offsets, and a healthy
appetite for food. Aside from his visits to us, he was starving and being
moody in Westport, temporarily out of girls. He drove back and forth
in a dark green MG TD that went well with his pipe.

His initial conviction was that I should learn lofting. I volunteered
to let him do it, but no way. So I rented a floor sander, scuffed all the
varnish off the pine floor of our dining room, first taking the table down
to the cellar and moving the chairs to various inconvenient locations.
Next, while he smoked and instructed, I laid out with steel tape, battens, and weights all the lines of the Gosling, and once that was
completed, I painted them in rainbow colors on the floor.

Before we began construction, we varnished the floor with two
coats of good spar (nothing cheap under the Baker eye). Bob assured

me that the completed dinghy could be carried out of the dining room, negotiating the right angle into the front hall around the radiator, and out the door. I believed him. Nobody else did. As we filled the room with the building frame, the pile of Honduras mahogany 3″ × 3/16″ strips (we were using the Ashcroft method), the clamps, the tools, the bucket of copper tacks, the bucket of copper washers, and the roll of plans, the general notion that we were building ourselves into a corner gained universal acceptance and generated smug jests.

The Ashcroft method, as Bob explained it, was really simple. The molds are set up crosswise of the building frame, and heavy stringers are set into them lengthwise, transom to stem. The stem and false keel are fitted outside everything, as is a solid transom (I had resisted Bob's suggestion that we set up a curved transom and Ashcroft a skin over it as preliminary training; too time-consuming). Then an initial layer of diagonal strips is bent around and fastened lightly to the frame, at forty-five degrees to the keel. A second layer is tacked, clenched, and glued over the cracks in the first layer. The copper tacks, plank by plank as you go, are turned inside over small washers. Then a final layer is clenched and glued over the first two, the last layer at right angles to the first.

Baker having abandoned me to the planking task, I could generally con a student into sitting inside the boat while I pounded tacks to his backup from without. When no members of the Kane Avenue Regulars were present to drink Kitty's tea, eat toasted cheese dreams, and absorb the raisin, oatmeal, wholewheat, and magic cookies known to one and all by my young son's name for them as "Mommie Rocks," I'd fit planks ahead and pin them lightly in place against the next unwary visitor.

The boat went swimmingly, with Baker showing up two or three times a week, generally at mealtime, to smoke at me and watch. Occasionally, in the absence of volunteer escapees from study hall, he'd pound from the outside while I backed him from the inside. It was frightfully noisy in there. Baker and I finished it in a late frenzy one night because I had to fly off to a speech over the weekend, and anyway Bob wanted to see it all planked. I went off about noon the next day —I think it was to Cleveland.

Anyway, when I came home, there was the dinghy, building frame and all, in the front yard. It had been the "revolt of mother" all over again. She'd persuaded Bud Worthley, the building and grounds superintendent, to take out the dining room double windows, frames and all, and park the boat on sawhorses in the front yard. (Bud scheduled his own time, and thus was an open hunting ground for most of the faculty. He was an exceptionally friendly man.)

I called Baker up, and he arrived the next noon, just after my last class. He was filled with glee at this chance for a demonstration of high competence and style. I got inside, he worked outside, and we dismembered the frame, removing the vital screws in the order of their importance and wrenching out the stringers. It was a miracle; the boat came off the frame intact as a sturdy, elegant shape, the swing of her sheer a poem, now that the excrescences were gone. We set it on its bottom and admired our mutual labor. It was superior.

Bob grinned. "Let's put it back in the house," he said. I looked at the door, the right angle around the radiator, the mirror hung in the passage, and all that. "Let's; there's nobody here to see us." We picked it up, light as you wouldn't believe, and inserted the bow through the door and up the stairs to the left of the door. Then passing the stern under the bow, we marched the hollow of the hull around the radiator, carried the corner of the transom into the dining room, and eased the boat after it, on edge. Everything cleared everything by half inches. We went back outside and brought in the sawhorses. When Kitty returned, she emitted a piercing scream, and we had to reverse the process, this time attended by the full cadre of the Regulars, who helped us carry it into the shop. I sanded it, painted it French Gray with a white bottom and a red boot top, and Bob carved "BOBTAIL" into the transom in elegant incised romans. I constructed the rig with laminated spruce masts and booms, laminated mahogany jaws, and laminated ash and mahogany blocks, striped. The rig turned out real purty.

The dinghy sailed like smoke. I remember a half gale in Nantucket Harbor, when I alternately screeched across the harbor on a wild plane, bailed my way to windward, and then did it again.

The resorcinol glue eventually delaminated in salt water (it holds well in fresh), and we fiberglassed the dinghy. My son used it for years,

I pose with my Gosling *below St. George's School.*

adding a jib and bowsprit to the cat rig. I last saw it under the gym at St. George's, where it still may be.

The spinoff of the dinghy was the Sprite, which we finally persuaded George O'Day to put into production. It took three visits, two of which generated in Baker only unwillingness and suspicion of O'Day. George is a Boston Irishman of Harvard football fame, great charm, and moderate wealth, an Olympic sailing champion, and handsome. Bob did not admire George's Olympic vehicle, a 5.5-meter sloop, as it had a flat sheer, a high aspect ratio rig, no room inside, and unlimited spinnakers, vangs, Cunninghams, downwind zippers, and suchlike. George's office had pictures of several of them, at which Bob ventured alternate looks and shudders, like a lady deliciously atingle at seeing a mouse.

My idea was a fiberglass trainer for St. George's that would be a bit more one-design than the home-built Puddleducks. It would be manned by a crew of two, or even three, for interscholastic contests. But as a trainer, it should begin as a one-man boat. We gave it two mast

steps, to start the neophytes in a cat. Once cause and effect was clear
to those soloing, we could move the mast back, add a jib, and give one
or two kids more strings to diddle. Finally, we gave them a lovely little
crosscut spinnaker, a pole, and more strings. To sell it to O'Day,
however, was against the grain. Bob's drawing of a broad, flat boat (a
child could walk around the gunwale without tipping it over, or getting
the transom in the teeth) with a rig that was both cat and sloop, let
alone a spinnaker to add expense, gave the buyer confusing options, and
was too small to make much speed difference—all this didn't wash.

But we were sold on the idea and Bob's beautifully designed shape.
I remember Olin Stephens remark that "naval architects have finally
gotten over their fear of beam." Bob never had it. Before our final trip
to O'Day, Bob had an inspiration; he made a lovely model of the
design, ten inches long, enchanting as a baby. It was planked up on
frames, and exquisite. He painted it different colors on different sides,
one pure white with a pencil-thin waterline, the other French Gray
with red boot top and white bottom. I phoned George, and we went
up. George fingered the model with the affection of a tasteful man for
a beautiful thing. "Bob," he said, "How much?" I butted in. "I want
the first ten free, for St. George's. You'll get a charitable deduction."

Bob diffidently asked, "What will you give me?" Money always
embarrassed him, coming in, that is. O'Day looked at him and said,
"I'll give you a choice—five thousand dollars or ten dollars a boat." Bob
was astonished. "I'll take the cash . . . ," he started, but I interrupted
and said he'd take ten dollars a boat. After the first thousand were sold,
he was still astonished. I hadn't really wanted O'Day to have time to
think about five thousand dollars and put off the building. St. George's
used the Sprites for four or five years and at the end of that time I
bought one from the school for $100, so my idea only cost me $100.

The model generated more business for Bob, and another unreal
relationship with reality. O'Day called him up one day and said, "Bob,
come on up here and bring your buddy Hoyt with you; I have a job
that will interest you both." We drove up in the windy little car, pipe
ashes streaming backwards, parked on Newbury Street, and climbed to
George's office. George unrolled the plans for a twenty-four-foot keel

centerboarder, the Dolphin, from Sparkman and Stephens. For a wonder, she was beautiful, even to Baker. She had a swing to the sheer, a tender bit of hollow in the bow, and a real personality—not soap-dish anonymity, and not the sort of character-boat overstyling that looks like a cross between a movie pirate ship and an Adidas sneaker.

"Bob," George said, "there's a boat show in a week and I need a model that shows the interior and the exterior by then. We're not building this unless we get at least ten orders. Can you do it?"

"Gosh George," Bob said, in a week? I'd have to work nights!"

"Right! Then it's a bargain?"

"O.K."

"Waaaaait a minute," I said, "what's the fee?"

"How do I know until I see the boat and Bob knows how many hours it took?"

I wondered why I was there, and soon found out. George had the idea that fiberglass hulls could be marketed with all the bits and pieces cut to fit at the factory, and the owner himself could do the expensive hand labor, thus preserving the profit and eliminating the Union. I was to buy a kit at cost from George, and rewrite his foreman's instructions to make the whole enterprise look like a piece of cake. We'd sell the instructions separately, possibly as a come-on. I said maybe. We drove home.

Four days later, after two phone calls from O'Day, who couldn't locate Bob for a progress report, Bob showed up in Newport, had a placid lunch without saying much, and then took me out to the car and showed me the model. He had gone to ground in Westport, taken the telephone off the hook, and gotten hooked by the model to the extent that he only dozed now and then. It was, of course, more affection-generating than the real boat could ever be, with an elegant eggshell finish and all the wee handrails, footrails, hatches, and trim in varnished mahogany. The wooden mast was bright, wire rigging with tiny turn-buckles. There was a wee working compass in the bridge deck. The winches on the mast and cockpit were aluminum pushpins, filed exactly to appropriate size. The deckhouse lifted up with the mast, and there was the interior, also white and varnished mahogany. The whole thing was on a wood base and chocked and blocked, as if it were in a boatyard. It was so great that I resolved then and there to have a real one. Actually, I needed a boat like poison ivy, having an extended membership in the Other People's Boat Club for two Transatlantic Races ahead. But even O.P.B.C. members need a boat to buy equipment for.

We called George, parked again on Newbury Street (after three times around the crowded block). I carried the boat upstairs as reverently as The Holy Grail, set it on George's desk, and sat down. Bob lifted the deckhouse. George tried it himself, with the awe with which a bachelor touches a baby. "Christ!" he said, "that's bea-oo-tiful!"

"How much?"

Bob looked diffidently at his feet. "Well George," he said, "I worked a lot at night."

"Come on Bob; name a price."

"Well, how's $250."

O'Day stood up. "Damn it Bob," he said, "you make me hate myself! I should give you exactly what you ask but that model is worth four times $250, at *least,* and I'm a businessman. I'm going to teach you a lesson. I'll only give you $500, unless you fight me."

"George," Bob said, "that's wonderful; I wouldn't fight you!"

Later, and for a solid fee that George suggested in advance, Bob made a half-model of the Dolphin for O'Day, and when it had gotten hurt in several boat shows, it came back to Bob for repair. It suffered the fate of all Bob's children that came back to him abused—he repaired it and retained it. Later, he gave it to me. I strongly suspect that the original was too nice to go to more than the first boat show and that it decorates the O'Day mansion.

By this time, Bob's orbit and mine had separated. He was designing boats and building them in Westport, writing them up with superb drawings and photographs for *Wooden Boat;* I was racing transatlantic, cruising with my full family, and lecturing two nights a week. I saw him, now and then, through the years. Again and again in *Wooden Boat,* I recognized the handsome Baker profile, the long body laid out reposefully in infinitely graceful little boats, pipe at the Roosevelt angle, negligent hand on the tiller. The picture always twanged at the heartstrings of my youth, when we argued about important things, like boats, not politics (he still believed in Roosevelt), not education.

I don't think that Bob's hands and Bob's mind ever created anything that wasn't beautiful. He has two fine sons I know and two more children I don't, but I can't forget Anna's comment on their ruptured marriage—"I should have gotten another child before I lost him." We all should have. His boats, his flawless children, will last a long time, like happy memories.

19

Behind the Bright Hours

NO OMENS WERE FAVORABLE. My crew—Tom, Bill, and John Buell, and Kitty Hoyt—had arrived in Bermuda two days behind my schedule to sail our *Telltale II* to Ireland. I'd been navigating the Bermuda Race, and had been 250 miles from Bermuda on Monday, 200 miles from Bermuda on Tuesday, and 178 miles from Bermuda on Wednesday. When I finally got there on Friday, Bert Darrell hadn't been able to haul our boat in the last six weeks, and she had hay on her bottom. By Monday I still had lists of things yet to be done. But all the Buells would run out of vacation unless we went. In St. George's, we managed to get a promise that the boat would be hauled, painted, and relaunched between morning and evening, but motoring around from Hamilton, Kitty smelled something peculiar. I opened the engine hatch on a disaster. The stainless (ha!) Aqualift had rusted out, and an hour's worth of salt-cooling water had joined lots of diesel exhaust in the bilge. A black mass of rusty water was rising over the starter and around the batteries. We anchored hastily, pumped earnestly, and finally had a dry engine room in random shades of tattletale gray. I next cut a length of retired firehose in half and hose-clamped it over the leak, reducing the flow to trickle, thus enabling us to power on. Five minutes later, the forepeak door sheared both hinges and fell with a prodigious clatter. We made the yard at noon and were hauled at 1300. By the next morning, a new Aqualift had been located and miraculously installed, the bottom was scrubbed and painted, the door was rehinged, and we were afloat, fueled and watered. It was noon.

From the town dock, Kitty, Tom, and John went ashore to collect more to eat and drink; Bill wound me aloft to check out the rig, install a spare halyard, and contemplate nature. To my horror, I found the masthead toggle for the headstay was hanging by one cheek, and that cheek was bent! To buy a new toggle was impossible; bending stainless is likely to fracture it. Nevertheless, I took the headstay down and did not discuss the peril with wife or crew. Instead, with the toggle against an oak billet and the dock, I whanged away at it with a stout hammer. To my ear, the steel continued to give out a tone sturdy and true until it realigned to fit the clevis pin. Half the solid toggle looked twice as strong as the stay, anyway, and I prayed that I had perfect pitch for steel tones. Then, all at once, Mr. Madeiros arrived with eighteen dozen eggs fresh from his hens, and a truck deposited my wife, the food, Tom, John, and the beer.

The yard bill still hadn't come, but I assumed I could send an appropriately large amount from Ireland or anywhere else. After all, it was my twenty-second trip across the Atlantic, and the big thing is to go, not stand on the order of your going; there's always more preparation and less courage if you're picky. We filled the junk bunk with food, raised sail at Mills Breaker Buoy, and watched Bermuda fade astern as we spinnakered into the sunset. Filled with serene assurance from past survivals and optimistic predictions from the meteorological office, we "lightly glided o'r the azure realm," at ease in Zion.

As skipper, rather than crew, you think a lot at sea, largely, thank heaven, to yourself. I assume that's what meditation is like, a sorting out. Gliding, I thought, "T'was not ever thus." For every blissful hour, there are a few minutes of numb misery, a few seconds of terror. But the first five days were idyllic—sunshine, the canopy over our heads by day, moonlit nights, dolphin and bos'nbird playing around us, and the cabin decorated for the Fourth of July feast.

On the evening of the fifth night, we were passed by the *Cardiff Clifford*, which for a wonder, was monitoring Channel 16 on the VHF. (During the crossing, we were passed by sixteen large vessels close to

Telltale's *crew: Bill Buell, Tom Buell, John Buell, and N.D.H. Kitty is the photographer.*

us. We called them all on Channel 16 and on 2182, and talked with five of them. So much for rescue if you yell "Mayday!") *Cardiff Clifford*'s position checked with ours, he received both our radios loud and clear, and he had just received a printout of the latest synoptic weather map. Boom! A cold front had developed between Hatteras and 150 miles north of the Azores, and a depression of 29.82 inches was moving along the front at (gulp!) thirty knots. Our plot put it half a day astern, with our position on the fast side. We could expect fifty-five or sixty knots.

At this point the halyard snap shackle let go, and we recovered the spinnaker over the bow before it touched water. It was already blowing twenty-five knots, so we stowed the pole, took down the main, set the storm trysail, and started reaching south under working jib and trysail.

The seas increased; the barometer exhibited a depressing tendency.

By midnight the wind was gusting above forty-five knots (the top of our wind gauge). The boat, under engine and storm trysail now, was making from six to twelve knots (top of speedo), depending on how we ran the wave faces. The cresting waves, now fifteen to twenty-five feet high and breaking into cascading tops, skittered the stern one way and another, and then dropped us into an abyss and cast the bow at the black pitch of midnight. We steered valiantly in half-hour shifts, broaching only once, and that momentarily. The broach threw us down against the port spray-dodger with enough force to bend two stanchions in, breaking one off. The spray, with fire-engine force, hosed the cockpit. Meanwhile the barometer continued to drop, and the moan of the wind in the rigging rose in pitch and tempo as the mast swung wildly across the sky. Bulky in rain gear, safety harnesses, and boots, we huddled in the cockpit and wordlessly entertained our private fears and plans.

It took me back to other storms, other disasters, all survived. In my private mind, I've always remembered the goodies of cruising—bright tropical beaches under palms, crystal waters jeweled with fish, the majesty of icebergs peppered with birds, the white villages on dark Greek islands, the slat-shadowed alleys of Spanish ports, the rain, trots, and pubs at Cowes, and the drink with the relieving watch of laughing fellow rovers before a peaceful night of easy running in the trades. But behind the bright hours, salting them with gratitude, are anxious nights followed by vicious slatting in great, leftover seas.

As raucous hour succeeded hour, I kept a face of calm assurance and dignity for the crew, yet a melancholy series of goofs ran persistently through my head. As a nautical expert, I've a great deal to be modest about.

There was the foggy day, for example, when I navigated with extreme care from Camden out of Penobscot Bay. I had tacked from buoy to buoy by the numbers and emerged into sunshine and open ocean to discover that on the chart I'd been in the inner channel, but I had actually negotiated the Muscle Ridge Channel. The American Buoy System is, of course, cunningly planned to frustrate reasonable people. Elsewhere in the world, one finds buoys with painted signs bolted to them reading "Kentish Knock," "Armen," or "Chebucto Head." But come from an American fog onto an American coastline and you're enlightened by "1" or "2."

Or there was the night when I was single-handing on a yawl without rail or lifelines and my haste to hoist the filling spinnaker led me to nimble backwards and overboard into Maine's icy waters, still clinging sincerely to the halyard, which, assisted by the spinnaker, towed me back to the boat. This cold bath diminished my confidence to the extent that I have never since set a sail at night without someone else on deck.

Sometimes past experience betrays rather than instructs. After three seasons of racing on *Bolero* with such superior hands as Corny Shields, Doc Davidson, Olin Stephens, Dick Goennel, Fred Lawton, Arnie Gay, Freddie Temple, and Bucky Reardon, I raced across the Atlantic on a German yawl, no member of whose crew, save Goennel and me, had ever set a spinnaker out of sight of land. The owner, a giant of a man with great charm, was an ex-*korvettenkapitain*, sunk three times on the Murmansk run. ("Norri, ven you go into de kalt vasser, take off only de shus. . . .") The navigator was an ex-*unterseebot* skipper. The rest of the crew was a feckless lot of hopeful adventurers and yacht-club fillers-in. The usual mid-Atlantic storm came on. "It struck us with o'ertaking wings and drove us east along."

We were down to a spitfire jib, wrung out on a spinnaker pole, a main reefed down to the numbers, and secret prayers. At such times I sing hymns to myself (twenty-eight years of required school chapel) like "Almighty Father strong to save . . ." and "Oh still small voice of calm . . ." The night was a roaring chaos of spray and wind. The boat, very fast when upright, was cascading along from hilltop to valley. Goennel and I were exchanging the helm every half hour, exhausted from cranking hard against her slew in an endless effort to keep the boat under the mast. When she heels and has only one side of the bow in the water, a boat going well above her designed speed broaches into disaster. Successful heavy weather running depends on keeping in balance.

We weren't really frightened until suddenly we were picked out, in the black exhaustion of 0200, by the searchlight of a large tanker

The goodies of cruising—Defiance off Little Tobago.

bound westward against the gale. She revealed herself, as her search-
light discovered us, with giant seas bursting over her bows, creaming
down 400 feet of deck, and breaking up and over her five-story island.
"Look," the spectacle said, "it's not just one wave at a time—the whole
damn ocean is marching!" By this time, Goennel and I were too tired
to steer any more, and our *Bolero* confidence in our fellows betrayed
us. We turned the helm over to Ulli Mahn, who had been O.K. in
normal running; ten minutes later he jibed her.

What a thorough disaster! The main-boom foreguy straightened
out its bronze snap hook and came across into the sea with a crash as
we broached; a giant sea fell on the boat and tore the mainsail out across
its reef points; the refrigerator came out of its nook in the doghouse
and rammed across the cabin to destroy part of the dish locker. The
owner summed up our unspoken consensus with the statement, "If I

had known it would be like this, I would not haf come!"

So, now, concentrating on *Telltale*'s wheel, or worse still, watching my friends in their busy energy as the black night roared on, I thought sadly of those hopeful souls who walk the streets of Newport before a Bermuda Race, advertising their availability as crew for any boat, with any skipper, their willingness to seek who knows what doom in the clamorous night. A line from *Lear* ran through my head, "We are but flies to the Gods . . ."

But now the barometer at 29.82 came sharply around the bend and started to rise. The seas continued to increase, and the wind blew on, but to different hearts. Absolution had been granted. Our helmsmanship improved with our spirits. Chastening, not judgment, had been visited upon us, and the dawn was just beyond the horizon. The great, anonymous bear paw of nature merely had been scratching its butt, indifferent to us. Somehow, indifference rather than an end to malice saves us from Fate, giving us back to ourselves and to each other.

Another squall swam into my memory. We'd been sailing to Guernsey from Falmouth in Guy Goodbody's *Kytra II*, designed for the OSTAR (The Observer Single-handed, Transatlantic Race), with twin running sails and vane steering. She's a delicious boat, runs like a deer, works well with her Hasler vane steering, and is beautiful besides—an Angus Primrose one-off. I had the deck, Goodbody was below with a sprained back (betraying his family name), and my wife was off watch and sleeping. Guernsey was just breaking the horizon, and the wind was light and aft, so I thought about it, saw how to set the twin running sails, and set them. They'd been up perhaps ten minutes when the wind over the deck picked up to twenty-five knots, and we began to make very brisk progress toward Guernsey's rocky shore. When we were five miles off, I went below and asked Goodbody how to get the running sails down. He quite simply replied that he'd never had them up.

What with two poles, four halyards, guys, sails, and sheets, I had a busy thirty minutes on the foredeck before I had everything stowed, and now Guernsey was a half-mile away, and we were approaching it with a reefed main and a small jib. It had been a bit close for my self-assurance, so, extra cautious, I got the anchor ready, rove sailstops into the boom, and struck the jib as we came through the great wall that encloses St. Peter Port.

Guernsey does not have the most commodious harbor in the world. It's about the size of four football fields with perhaps 100 yachts in it and some thirty-five feet rise and fall of tide. Some of it dries out, and some of it has great steamer docks, so what's left for a late arrival is limited. To my astonishment, there was a great open space in the middle, and single-handedly, I rounded up smartly, threw a stop on the dropped main, and cast the anchor exactly where I wanted it. I then fed out 250 feet of chain and settled back to the hook with the feeling of having put on a tidy show. The cocktail hour was in full swing among the other yachts, my rain gear said HOYT on the back, and my companions emerged to contemplate the scene as the harbormaster bumped alongside in his launch.

"Ye cawnt anchor here!" he said, broadly accented.

"And why not?" I asked.

"Because a bloody great steamer will come in tonight and sink you," he said, and rowed away. It was still blowing about twenty-five knots.

I started the engine, went forward to hand 250 feet of chain onto the deck, and felt diminished. As the anchor broke free, *Kytra II* drifted sideways, rather mulish about handling with forty feet of chain dribbling from its nose. She fetched up against several moored small boats. Kitty ran forward and leaned over to push off as I sweated away at the anchor with desperate energy. At the helm, Goodbody now tried to back away, but the boat was drifting and backing into still more boats and the whole spectator fleet was relishing a thorough muck-up when a voice rang into my consciousness: "Hoyt! Your bird's overboard!"

I turned around, and there was no sign of Kitty. I let go of the anchor and dashed to the bow. There she was, her glasses preserved by her upheld face and her hands now frantically climbing the descending anchor chain. I dove between the pulpit pipes and grabbed a hand, pulled it over the rail, put a foot on it to retain it, and reached over the pulpit to pull her aboard. One shoe was gone, but she was in otherwise good, if damp, shape. A round of applause sounded through the fleet. The customs inspector now arrived with a motor launch and two seamen, and we were ignominiously helped to a mooring and secured there with what struck me as an excess of kindly tolerance.

The debacle concluded, we elected to have our drinks out of attention, ashore, and proceeded to the yacht club, which was on the third floor of a waterfront building. I was greeted by a cordial "Thanks for the show, Hoyt" by a group standing around a giant set of German binoculars, tripoded in the window. Everyone bought us drinks, and we were taken off to dinner by a delightful gentleman named Charles Graves (brother of poet Robert and himself author of a thoroughly documented, ironic book called *Europe on 5000 Pounds a Day*).

It's always a delightful transition from the mute intransigence of the inanimate to the warmth of friendship. Next morning, in mid-Atlantic, as the barometer rose and we fell about in a great windless swell and a sunny day, and the batteries tested low from a night of running lights, and the engine wouldn't start because of the water we'd got in it when the Aqualift let go, I went to musing again. I considered our innocence in the hands of fortune, our blind dependence on each other on the sea's face. The skipper's decisions have to be right, and we must have faith; the navigator has to know where he is, and we must have faith. My crew, our friends, our guests, slept through their off watches, calmly confident that I'd get them to Ireland.

Years ago, on *Xanadu II*, we approached Ireland at the end of a Transatlantic Race, no sights for the last three days in a solid fog, the whole lot blindly dependent on my navigation. Despite inner qualms, I did not quite feel I could say, "Sorry, chaps, but our position is uncertain and we'd better heave to until it clears." So we rushed on, through darkness at noon, and I reviewed all the courses and speeds they had said they'd done. When I finally picked up Mizen Head on the RDF, I found our bearing ran directly through Fastnet Rock, to which our DR course was laid. I went forward to fend off, but we never saw it, never heard its "cannon in fog." When the glue lifted, hours later, we were exactly on our dead reckoning position off the Old Head of Kinsale. It was one of the mysteries of the sea.

Or there was the time when we came in on Bermuda in the screaming gale of the '72 race with the fathometer packed up, and both RDF stations on the wrong side of the island and virtually useless. Reefed to the numbers and thundering through the seas, the night black, I felt the seas changing their characteristic from the regular weight of deep water to the pitched seas of shoaler waves. We were on the reef-strewn north side of the island, and we tacked. An hour later the seas were massive again, and we tacked back toward Bermuda, danger, and the finish. In thirty tense minutes Kitchen Shoals blinked ahead, and we rounded for the barn. Cruising, I'd have hove to and waited for daylight; but racing, the faith of the crew, and their companionable efforts made me reach deeper, persist, cope. Even with but slender evidence at hand, one must cope.

So there was no point in wailing about the starter; we just had to get on with it. I got the starter off the engine, disassembled it, dosed it with penetrating oil and CRC, and loosened the bound bearing with a Stilson wrench, effort, and two hours work. The batteries had regenerated a bit, and the starter (barely) started the engine. In the little world of voyaging you take it as it comes and go on to the next stage, moving along on your small island of self-sufficiency, of faith, of experience.

With a thousand miles to go we had another storm, less severe, but busy, and another calm, and finally, as the wind went ahead to a close reach and came in cold, it gave us three fall-clear, dark-skied days with brilliant sunshine. The seas were modest, and at eight knots we raced toward Ireland, gradually finishing off the last three bottles of rum at high-noons and evenings, and sailing joyously. A school of six or seven dolphin came leaping across the waves from starboard and joined us for most of a day—absolutely zestful beasts. One frequently leaped vertical into the air, looked us over, and tumbled sideways into the sea. Another came in hell-bent from port, leaped in a long arc six inches off the pulpit, and plunged cleanly into the water at starboard.

Watching them, I thought of my zestful companions from the years past, shipmates who had loved the sea and sailed their last voyage, enthusiasts all. I saw them reincarnated in these joyous creatures, rollicking along in the bright sea—Blunt, Bill, Max, Bruce, Hank, Curtis greeting mariners with the certain assurance that existence is a continuing wonder.

Two days later we were in Crosshaven, County Cork, and our friends bade us a briefly emotional farewell and went back to the regular world, where experience is less immediate, to cope in their various ways with the day to day, this trip added to the rich mine of memory.

ATLANTIC CROSSING

for NDH

Knuckles nut tight on the wheel,
running my mantra like an outboard.
Like the time I'd fallen in, alone,
in the middle of the pond, breaking
my way to the edge.

I'll make it home, I'll make it sure,
running there with skates still on,
over the frozen fields.

Or the first time I prayed,
my white rat lying senseless
on the bed from hitting him hard
with a sockfull of BB's because
he'd half eaten the starling I'd
saved, fallen from its nest.

(The rat, righting itself, blinked pink.)

And you, the skipper, tallest teller
of any tale, you were speechless
in the banshee night, storm try'l set,
running before a full gale, and I
needing blather to keep my mind
from broaching, pitchpoling, giving in.

My mantra half in gear now and slipping,
over the edge, and you, the skipper
catatonic. But no, (TE DUM!)
you gray beard loon, you were asleep.
Half awash but sleeping. If you
could have that much faith,
then I could too, and tell the tale.

— T. C. BUELL

20

Total Immersion

AMONG THE MANY DELIGHTS OF cruising, getting wholly into the local scene involves all the moves of making a career in one's own home town. You move in modestly, meet an old friend who's been there a little longer, get introduced around, and gradually, being new on the scene, achieve upward mobility. The sailor has great advantages —a short stay (limited involvement), new anecdotes, and fashionable clothes (Newport being more with-it than, say, Gibraltar). Then, having drunk and dined with the great and near-great, you acknowledge permanent indebtedness to them and their community and sail off into the blue, warm with cordial memories.

I love Gibraltar. It's the staging point for Europe-to-the-Caribbean voyagers; it's a last bastion of proper Brits; and it's a free port, and thus an acquisition mecca for dumpy Russians, wily Mideast types, and cooing ladies with purple coiffures, newly released from cruise ships, shopping ecstatically. Liptons will give an embarking yachtsman a discount of 10 percent on everything discountable, will deliver the whole to the marina or sub-pens, and will take a check. Booze can be bought, tax-free, at close to wholesale (wines at little more). Ice, now, is more of a problem. The local fish-freezery vends, in washbasin-shaped discs, block ice that won't park well in square refrigerators. One acquires these lumps, one at a time, and carries them, while they melt, back to the sub-pens. So I bought two large, square plastic buckets, and, after a brief battle with the language barrier (Maltese?), managed to persuade the fish-freezer that ice could be made in something with a handle.

But I rush ahead of my narrative. We'd been to Gibraltar thrice before, once by bus, and twice by sail. We came by bus with Curtis Bok after *Alphard*'s mast collapsed off Trafalgar Bank while beating to windward in a small wind with a large jib and a larger head sea. One of the four mid-mast tangs let go. The mast compressed and twisted downwards in a gentle spiral before we could let the sheet go and round up. Relieved, it straightened and split helically, the way you embrace a slim girl, the left hand waist to hip, the right hand chest to shoulder. We bound it with battens and rope, and motored back into Cádiz, the fracture grunching against itself with noises more torturous to the nerves than broken bones. The drive, two days later, to Gibraltar was frying hot, with the lumpy landscape out the dusty window vibrating in thermal waves. The bus dropped us in Algeciras, where, from an airy balcony looking at the Rock, we were served icy gaspacho and since we now felt adventurous, pulpo.

All our mail for two months was waiting for us in Gibraltar, with the U.S. Naval Attaché, who, when called, sniffily informed us that we couldn't come up at once as he was hosting "some VIPs." Since all importance is relative, I insisted we compare merit badges. The VIPs turned out to be "the American ambassador to St. James and a naval architect called Olin Stebbins." Mr. "Stebbins," when summoned to the phone, gleefully invited us to our mail; Winthrop Aldrich, whose sister's portrait Kitty had painted, kissed her in the doorway; we were launched in Gibraltar.

Wayfarer, a Sparkman-and-Stephens-designed, ninety-foot center-board yawl, was being rewired by the British Naval Establishment, having been wired in an involuted way by Abeking and Rasmussen. A short circuit in the autopilot had knocked the captain flat on his back and eliminated electrical continuity. We were given a grand tour of the boat, admired the bathtub, the hi-fi in gimbals (ready to play "Rock Around the Clock"), and were awed by a wooden mainmast we could not get our arms around and snatch blocks the size of my chest. We forthwith experienced total acceptance in Gibraltar; we were given a military tour of the gun emplacements in the Rock; we were photographed with monkeys on our heads; we dined with the admiral and drank at the "Oldest Yacht Club in the World" as guests of the commodore and reciprocated hospitality at Curtis's suite at the Rock Hotel. We flew home, full of ourselves, practically Old Rock Hands.

Fourteen years later we were there again, with *Kytra II*, on our way to Malta. Since onward, rather than upward, mobility was our aim, we had recourse to agent Charley Rodriguez, friend to generations of sailors, in Horsebarracks Lane. While he rounded up everything we needed, we watched a British Military Band, dressed in kilts and leopard skins, do a full-court performance through the streets to the Parade. We had drinks with Commander Codrington, C.O., on (Her Majesty's) cruiser, and were bemused to find a small but superb Corot in one lighted alcove and a well-anchored T'ang horse in another. (I thought of writing a brief piece for *Connoisseur* on "The Effect of the Battle of Jutland on the World's Art Collecting.") That evening we dined in Algeciras and enjoyed two marvelous young flamenco dancers. The next morning we left for Malta with full stores and spares.

Our fourth trip was on our own *Telltale II*, both ways. We arrived in a condition of breathless gratitude. The weather, after an easy passage from Ireland, became too much for the two of us. Gales pinned us in to La Coruña for twelve days, while indigent innocents in tiny boats, ill equipped, borrowed our Read's Sailmaker sewing machine and consumed pounds of thread. Canvas repaired, they'd venture foolishly out of shelter and return for more stitching. My own impatience finally peaked, and we made a rugged, storm-trysail reach to Vigo Bay, enjoyed the Club Nautico at Bayonna a week, and caught a half gale down to Cádiz, where we waited out another gale in its sooty, oily harbor. Then, the weather breaking clear and mild, we reached to Cape St. Vincent, sharpened, and finally beat into Gibraltar in bright sunlight with gusts, the Rock streaming its levanter banner of cloud.

Gibraltar had been readied for us. Our good friends in Newport, Ted and Barbie Sturtevant, annually gave fall, Christmas, and spring parties for the foreign officers at the Naval War College to introduce them to social and naval Newport outside their classroom orbit. Reciprocally, officers from everywhere urged the Sturtevants to send their traveling friends toward naval outposts and home stations. The Sturtevants, fearing we might be shy of pressing ourselves on minor acquaintances, had written ahead. Our week in Gibraltar escalated socially. Rear

Admiral and Mrs. Firth, he a bulky sea dog, she a slightly sultry and remarkably beautiful woman, had notes awaiting us at the dock, and they took us to cocktails. A day later, friends of ours from the States, the Harrises, arrived, introduced us to everybody at the marina, and the Firths took us all for lunch at the swimming club. By this time we were socially launched. We saw everything on the Rock, were given history books, were taken to the Chart Repository and had our navigational charts fleshed out. We took folk to lunch at curry and Asiatic emporia, and we stocked the boat. Before the Firths left for a new assignment and we left for the Balearics, they gave a dinner party for twenty at a cave near the Catchments. Inundated by hospitality, we left Gibraltar feeling like royalty—overfeted, but undeniably loved.

We continued to find that cruising foreign parts could be a succession of sociable delights. After cruising the south coast of Spain and up around the Cabo de Gata to the Balearics with a succession of friends, we sailed back around Spain to Puerto José Banus, whose lighthouse, now the administration building, symbolically had been built by Algerian pirates. This incredible complex of marina berths, hotels, restaurants, shops, swimming pool, movie theater, and bull ring were erected by and named after a latter-day pirate, a supporter of Franco, and thus his own immortalizer.

We contracted to winter there, tied stern-on to a massive dock just 100 yards from the theater, and I spent a busy two days laminating arced mahogany sides to support a gangplank, while Kitty discovered *Hyper,* sort of a K-Mart-cum-Supermarket, where Rioja wines were about thirty-five cents a bottle, by the case. The theater showed English-speaking movies every Wednesday night—a most sociable occasion. The seats were individual upholstered armchairs, the lobby bar was open before the performance and at half time, and everybody who was anybody came. At our first attendance, Robin Somerville, a wild spirit from Australia and London, who was the ex-wife of an old friend, greeted us with hoots of pleasure and enveloped us in hospitality. Within days, we were part of the British drinking and divorcing community, attending entertainments ranging from parties around the pool to luncheon at a restaurant catered by a gay couple for the Irish Sweepstakes, at which the local Episcopal chaplain conducted his own sweepstakes for the benefit of the church. There would have been more benefit with less champagne.

I fell in with Fred Hess, who ran a yacht-broker supply shop, and we had occasional sails on his demonstrators with putative customers. We drove and picnicked in the hills, and visited the Alhambra with Robin and her Colonel, Guards, Retired. Since Puerto José Banus was a showplace, we met the Niefosh family, whom we later visited in Burlington, Vermont, and the Bibbs, whom we next saw in Carmel, California. Since it's almost impossible to cash a check in Spain, we got money by advertising our need at parties, where we could beat the exchange rate with any check that could be mailed to a Swiss bank. Once, having rounded up $700 worth of pesetas on my way to Marseilles for a race, I had to smuggle them out of and back into Spain in my shoes, since only token sums of native specie could cross borders. All in all, Puerto José Banus showed us the expatriate way of life in depth.

But the time had come to head back to the Caribbean and start our world cruise. Our seventies were creeping up on us, and later would be too late. We acknowledged our eternal indebtedness to the Banusians and sailed off into the blue—Gibraltarwards, to meet Jean and Avery Seaman for the ocean crossing.

The Sturtevants had been in touch with us during the winter, and their great friends and buddies, Captain and Mrs. Walker, of the Royal Navy, were in residence at Rosia Parade, Gibraltar. We sailed the thirty miles to Gibraltar and tied up again in the sub-pens, outboard of a great greasy fishing boat rebuilding its engines. Ave and Jean arrived. The weather prediction was great for a crossing. The Walkers came down and had drinks with us, and invited us to dinner the next evening. We set about ordering from Charley Rodriguez, Liptons, and a liquor importer. Then, late in the afternoon, I marched the hot mile to the icemaker and brought back my second pair of square ice blocks. Kitty was putting on her finest clothes for our dinner date and had laid out my double-breasted British yachting jacket, my RORC necktie, gray flannels, and a white shirt. The fridge loaded against the morrow, I showered in the cockpit, dried, and was below dressing when, simultaneously, the Walkers' station wagon arrived to collect us all, and the

Liptons' van arrived with crates of food, some perishable. I sent everyone ahead to front for me while I stuffed it away, and the official driver agreed to return.

I was showering again when the car returned, and I dressed damply. Locking the hatches, I stepped over our lifelines and onto the heavy rubbing strake of the fishing boat, just as a surge rocked it against the dock and my foot slipped. In full kit, I rocketed between boats, surfaced soggily, and splashed my way astern to the greasy dockside ladder. Dripping mournfully, I looked at the driver, and he looked at me. "They're 'avin' their secon' drink roight nah, Sa," he said. "You could loie dahn in back, orf the seats." It seemed like a temporary solution.

Dubiously, I knocked at the door in Rosia Parade, standing in my own puddle. "I slipped," I said. Captain Walker grinned from ear to ear. "Wow!" he said. "Go around back and I'll meet you." He led me through the kitchen, bringing the preparation of splendid platters of food to a full halt while the Oriental staff gaped, and he showed me to a shower. "Shower in all your clothes," he instructed, "and I'll bring you hangers and a bathrobe." To the staff he said, "We'll have another round of drinks."

I arrived in the living room in a woolly gray bathrobe, and instantly had a captive audience. Walker stepped to my side, put his hand on my shoulder, paused for silence, and announced, "This is Norry's fifth visit to Gibraltar. He's become totally immersed in our way of life."

We had a crown roast of lamb for dinner. I've never been hungrier. It tasted remarkably better than harbor water.

21

Show and Tell

THERE IS more than a little ham in every schoolmaster, and I am less than an exception. The earmarks of hamminess are easily recognized in the abrupt change of tone, from roar to confidential; the meticulous pronunciation of each syllable; the throw-away line; the understatement sneaked in before the shocker; the pause prolonged in mid-flight. After all, to be effective in the classroom you have to get the little scapers' attention. But effectiveness in the classroom is intoxicating, and like intoxication, it leads to addiction. I can only plead in extenuation that my previous addiction to sailing seduced me into after-dinner speaking. Speaking, in turn, involved me in both comedy and triumph.

My career as a public figure began innocently enough. We had sailed in the new American ambassador to Norway's yawl, *Pavana*, to Bergen, and had spent the weeks before he arrived wandering past waterfalls, up fjords, and through ancient Hanseatic League ports. We took yards of Kodachrome. Then, back at home base, like every born-again Columbus, we showed and told. We invited friends to dinner, abused their critical faculties with liquid hospitality, and broke out the slide projector. My good wife, lulled by my so-familiar voice, invariably sloped off into slumber, thus freeing me from a meticulous attention to exact fact.

A teacher's most basic instinct is audience awareness—once you lose them, you have to talk louder, or open a window, or change the subject. Even among bemused friends, I sensed which slides and which related remarks in my living-room show-and-tell excited patience, and

excised them from the repertory. Thus, from the great excess, I filtered
down slides and chatter to an effective performance. It was a heady
experience, after years of one-shot shows in the classroom, where my
lead balloons were many. I discovered the exhilaration of a choreo-
graphed, surefire, bang-on show. Catnip! And the Freudian slip here,
the inspired remark there, slowly added themselves to the bit.

My big break came when the program chairman of the Trinity
Church Discussion Group, desperate for intellectual rain (however
thin) in a dry season, asked me to "Do It in Public" for his lot. I was
never better; it was a Finished Performance! Better still, from the point
of view of church groups, it was free, and I thus became a popular
speaker. I generally got a covered-dish supper out of it, and in the
high-rent districts, preliminary cocktails in a private home. These
added to the exuberance of my verbosity.

Meanwhile, fully employed as a schoolteacher with a stack of daily
themes to correct, a sailing, swimming, or photographic gang to coach,
a yearbook and a dormitory to supervise, and faculty meetings and
meals to attend, I set a policy of only two evenings out a week. I thus
turned down an occasional invitation to speak.

Our headmaster, the Reverend Bill Buell, at least as much of a ham
as I was, had a marvelous habit of mildly emitting blockbusting remarks. When the captain of the football team stalked imperiously into
the Tuck Shop and ordered an Eskimo Pie by loudly demanding a "shit
on a stick," he heard behind him his headmaster's voice, "Make it
two." Bill never cursed, or even got excited. Thus I was considerably
surprised one morning when he grasped my arm, pulled me into his
office, and said, "These damned Churches!" It transpired that I had
refused to speak for an overzealous program chairperson whose schedule, she felt, was more demanding than mine. She had called the
headmaster to compel him to order his minion into line. "Norry," he
said, "we can't have you making enemies for The School." My jaw
dropped. "I could quit these talks," I said. "Oh no, no, no! Just
overcharge them! Then they'll respect you. You can always diminish
your popularity by raising your price." He was wholly right, and his
advice substantially helped my children through boarding school and
college. As I became greedy, I learned that, if the audience was to be

Hoyt explains the gale that died too soon to the Stamford "Soup and Sloop."

mixed, my price could not be higher than an orchestra's, because wives prefer dancing to sea stories.

The after-dinner speaker soon learns certain tricks of his trade. Seated at the head table, he is surrounded by the *éminences grises* of the organization. By exploring their backgrounds and listening closely to conversations between them, the speaker can pick up enough familiarity to throw a few humorous shafts into his hosts and thus delight *hoi polloi*. He husbands a few sharp jokes about long-windedness to start his talk, thus castigating preliminary over-verbose treasurers, secretaries, and other procedural persona who (microphone-intoxicated) lengthen the program toward those hours when the baby-sitter has to be returned to base. Protest does no good at the time; you hope it may help next year. But no matter how skilled at shortening the program, at amusing your listeners, and at wolfing the chicken-à-la-king, there's a long drive home after the clapping.

I think the only night I ever got home at a reasonable hour was when the Woonsocket Power Squadron asked me to speak at a joint dinner with the Attleboro Power Squadron. When I arrived, the program chairman took me aside and confessed, with some embarrassment, that Attleboro (if my memory serves me) had also scheduled after-dinner entertainment. Unperturbed, I allowed as how I could be on the quick side, or could enjoy their dinner and company, and be an audience. He said that the other side had agreed to shorten their act, and everyone wanted both shows—did I want to be first or second? Mindful of the old vaudeville adage, "never follow a dog act," I asked what the other show-and-tell was? "It's more show than tell," he said. "It's a striptease." Embellishing nothing, I left out half my slide trays and was in bed before midnight. I hope their ecdysiast was pertly perfect.

I will omit here the details of the hundred-car pileup on Route 128 that made me a little late for a talk to the Massachusetts MORC, or the drive home, intermittently interrupted by cops, with one headlight shining straight up. I'll skip the night when, starting late for an evening speech, I bit into a breast-of-pheasant sandwich Kitty had lightly wrapped in a paper napkin. In the dark, and on a cold winter's night, I didn't feel the napkin in time, and I spent the first ten miles getting it out of my teeth, off the roof of my mouth, and out of the toast and pheasant. I'll pass over the night at Marblehead High School when a helpful friend, handing me a fifty-five-slide box, dropped it on the floor and together, to save time, we put the slides back in any old which way. I projected them, said the line for each slide without any logical sequence, and enjoyed the entire audience's craning their necks right, left, and upside-down while they laughed uproariously. I was accused of doing it purposely for the laughs. Actually I'd felt nothing but a cold sense of disaster until I realized that once they're laughing, they'll laugh at anything. Once you get a reputation for early rising, you can sleep till noon.

Sometimes the disaster factor in my show-and-tell did not strike until late in the day, and it wasn't always my ineptitude. During most of my lecturing years, I had a houseful of women (a wife, and two daughters) to make life more interesting. One of their unbreakable habits was to drive the car until the gas gauge hovered toward extinction, and then to use the other car, thus sticking me with the financing. At this point we had a diesel and a gas Mercedes, both previously owned bargains because the American Blue Book downgraded foreign car prices. The diesel, although I did not know it, was hovering on the brink of disaster. While we were away for the summer, we had lent it to my nephew who, influenced by movies and folklore, shifted up and down incessantly, used the engine as a screaming brake, and in general acted like the Nouvolari of New Haven, Connecticut. Since a diesel fires on compression, braking with the engine results in preignition and repeated trauma to the crankshaft. But enough of this preamble to a tale.

It was late in January, and I had given a severe lecture to my older daughter, Katy, about not treating her mother with considered impatience. Paternal duty done, I drove to Boston, did my thing, and flushed with success, applause, and flattery, drove cautiously home through a thin snowfall. Seventeen miles from home, as I crossed the bridge at Tiverton, there was a horrid bang in the engine compartment, the wheels locked, and we skidded. I pushed in the clutch and coasted in to the curb; the crankshaft had broken. In the slowly growing cold of a wintry two o'clock in the morning, I listened to the engine tick as it cooled. A flashlight at my steamed-up window brought me out of the half-sleep of despair. "Ya can't park here, mister," said the local patrolman. "I can't go, either," I replied. Only getting out, lifting the hood, and having him contemplate the leaning flywheel with his flashlight convinced him. He called the State Police, who arrived, flagged the car, and took me to the Portsmouth Barracks. It was halfway home, and there they called Kitty and left me in an empty room. Much later, I remembered that I had driven the diesel because the other car was very nearly empty.

At a pay phone, I called Kitty; too late! Katy said she'd already left, then said, "Oh God! The sink's running over!" and hung up. Ten minutes later, the duty officer informed me my wife was out of gas at a closed Getty station and would be driven home, with me, by one of his troopers. "Mac," he said, "don't do nothin' else tonight."

While all this was happening, Katy was bleeding. She had turned off the TV when her mother left, filled the sink, squirted soap on the dishes, and turned on the hot water vigorously. While she talked to me, the sink overflowed. Barefoot, and in haste, she skidded on the wet linoleum, rocketed under the sink, and smashed two gallons of cider with her feet. Frightened and bleeding from both feet, she abandoned her station for the sofa, where, her feet wrapped in newspaper, she was still sobbing hopelessly when Kitty and I returned. Our friendly trooper, in order to write a brief report for me to sign, followed me to the disaster area. After I comforted Katy, I suggested he might like a drink. "Mac," he said, "I can't drink on duty, but believe me, you sure need one!"

If only I'd taken pictures! The whole story was so great I yearned to work it into a show, but who'd believe it without slides?

22

The Joys of Inconsistency

THE LIFELONG SAILOR is offered such a variety of choices that, like Brigham Young, he must now and then pause to wonder where love lies. From small beginnings in sailing classes, charter cruising, family boating, or just reading up an appetite in the extensive library of ultimate storms, legendary circumnavigations, and perfect ships, he progresses to day racing or gunk-holing, to ocean racing or coastwise cruising, to passagemaking, to designing, buying, building, or even brokering. Some of us find one or the other of these operations a terminal addiction, an area whose horizons expand infinitely. Others, vacillating like children in a candy shop from temptation to temptation, experience various plateaus in the learning process, and emerge, resolved at last, serene in a single love.

Some day I hope it will happen to me. I've been a split sailing personality for too long. Driving by a tidal marsh or a mountain lake, I itch to sail in it; cruising, I have a needless impulse to change sails and race strangers; racing, I yearn toward horizon-distant harbors.

When I was about twelve, I learned to sail in a Barnegat Bay sneak box, a blunt-ended shooting punt with a gunter rig, crowned deck, and centerboard. It was wet, tender, and over-rigged for my sixty-five pounds, but when it capsized, I could stand up in the lagoon northeast of Watch Hill, Rhode Island, my sailing ground. When I got the mast out of the eelgrass, I was off again. The joy of my solitary command, gliding through wind and water, was enough. I was a summerlong addict.

I was taught to swim that fall, won my first race a week later, and abandoned sailing for daily miles in the pool, meets all over the country, intercollegiate records, national championships, and total dedication. Late in my collegiate career, I re-encountered sailing, in the person of Frank Bissell and his winning yawl, *Dorothy Q*. Like an AA who rediscovers The Drink, my addiction blossomed, and I spent the summer after my graduation again afloat as tutor companion to the prolific Ballard tribe on Chebeague Island, in Casco Bay, Maine. The Ballards had a thirty-eight-foot yawl, a thirty-six-foot sloop, a twenty-foot sloop, and lesser craft. Guest days were proportionately allotted to the older children through the long summer. We day sailed, took weeklong cruises by pooling guest days, slid to vague anchorages in the light airs of moonlit nights, and sailed to and from shopping expeditions to Portland, eight miles away. We sailed into Cape Porpoise through thirty cords of lobster buoys; we came out of the fog at Squirrel Island and into the pointed firs of Boothbay; we circumnavigated most of Casco Bay's 365 islands, swatted giant mosquitos in The Basin, and beat out past Little Mark against wind and current. In retrospect, this intensive exploration of the immediate environment seems to be the very epitome of cruising, free of the sins of haste, of rising early to Get There, of sailing beyond the sunset of pleasure.

But I was young, hungry, and more willing to see than to experience. The planted seed of cruising waited to germinate while I raced: raced to Bermuda, to Annapolis, from Annapolis, raced in the P.R. Roosevelt Trophy Races, the Stamford-Vineyard, the New York Yacht Club Cruise, the Twenty-hundred, and lesser fixtures. The vessel for these adventures was the *Bolero*, a local seventy-three footer of some note. She had a good cook, a captain, two professional crew, and for serial events like the Cruise, a fifty-foot tender to bring along the champagne and artichokes.

Even under such favorable circumstances, the sailing was athletic. Routine demanded that we stop up every sail immediately after we changed down or up, and that we change from the light number 1 genoa to the heavy number 1, and thence to the number 2, number 3, number 4, number 5, and finally to the number 2 jib top and staysail. We naturally set the staysail before every change. I still remember the

number 5 genoa without affection, all 400 wet pounds of it, as our chain
gang, fatigued by four sail changes in a watch, hauled it from the
cockpit locker where it lived and yoicked it along the weather rail to
where Captain Lawton or Freddie Temple hanked it to the headstay.
Three or four of us, once relieved of its burden, tailed the halyard, and
up she rose on the run.

Sail changes in those dark ages of canvas were always all-hands calls,
and the foredeck, bucking into a head sea at nine to eleven knots, rose
ten feet in the air, dropped out under you, and dove through three feet
of the next wave before again rising. The force of the water peeled your
oilies up your legs, elastic and all, and filled your boots.

On the other hand, it was Lucullan Luxury below. Meals were
served in two sittings, on what are now known as "personalized" gear.
The owner's flag, crossed with the NYYC burgee, the boat's name, and
a gold ring were around all dinnerware. The same were enameled on
tableware, embroidered on towels, napkins, tablecloth, sheets, pillow-
cases, and washrags. The galley, with "Old White Joe," the cook, was
wrapped around the mainmast, and the professionals entertained themselves by trying to sleep still farther forward, where the action was. We
sybarites in the Corinthian crew rested elegantly in the pilot berths and
settees of the main salon while the command contingent (Corny
Shields, Doc Davidson, Olin Stephens, and J. N. Brown, the owner,
dozed in staterooms aft of our downy nests. The yacht's twenty-eight
tons rode so smoothly through tumultuous seas that we rested placidly,
securam in tempestate, insulated from wind and wave. I recall one night
when the wind had risen over thirty knots, and we were adding our ten
knots to it. Olin came below, snapped on the overhead lights, and
remarked reflectively, "From the peace and quiet that reigns here
below, you get no conception of the emergency of the situation on
deck." And out we went.

Unfortunately, the cook retired, Captain Lawton was stolen by
Raytheon, and *Bolero* was sold. Having paid my dues to Neptune under
Lawton's ungentle tutelege, I had acquired an addiction to racing and
passagemaking, and managed, in the next twenty years, some twenty
crossings of the Atlantic, in addition to various races on a variety of
craft. I gradually eased aft from the foredeck to the winches, from the

winches to the helm and decision-making in the cockpit, and finally, below, to the navigator's slot. I had even picked up a little cooking, under Bill Snaith's hand, in preparation for a senior citizenship through which, *mutatis mutandis,* I could cook my way from race to race without ever shedding my carpet slippers. I was a raceaholic, swilling horizons.

However, what with having a wife, a thirty-two foot cutter, and three children, I occasionally slipped into cruising between races and passages. After ten years, Kitty and I sold the cutter, not using it enough. This gesture brought us to a year in which nobody I knew was going transatlantic, so I acquired a twenty-six foot, twin-bilgeboard, hot-molded sloop designed by Uffa Fox, an Atalanta, from G. O'Day. It weighed two tons on its trailer, and I dedicated its year to my family. But my initial approach, in line with Rod Stephens dictum "I cruise at ninety percent of racing efficiency" lacked contemplation. Christmas vacation, even from a boarding school, is a bare three weeks, and it's a long way to sunshine from December in Newport, Rhode Island. With two tons of trailer-boat behind a half ton of car with a quarter ton of dunnage and a contract to write a pictorial article, I was obliged to preserve the visual purity of the all-white Oldsmobile I had borrowed from General Motors. The highways were rainy, and I washed the boat and trailer and car every time the sun hit us in the sand barrens of New Jersey, the pine flats of the Carolinas, the palms of Winter Park, the orange groves of. . . .

In four days we were launched in Florida's Biscayne Bay, still panting. We explored Biscayne Bay until a norther killed the poinsettias, went across to Fort Meyers and circumnavigated Sanibel Island, and heading north, left the boat with a friend in Tennessee.

The Easter vacation was less frantic. We launched the boat in Vicksburg and went down the Mississippi for *McCall's,* the magazine of low cleavages and "togetherness." Alerted to the need for "reader identification," we did lots of things our readers could do without a boat. *McCall's* had alerted all Chambers of Commerce from Vicksburg south to be aware of our arrival and that millions would read of our adventures. Their resulting hospitality made us conscious that our readers could eat themselves oblate in various caravanserais, tour stately mansions, visit battlefields, and attend pageants. My female children were stuffed into pantaloons and ruffled skirts and paraded with authentic you-alls in the Natchez Pageant; my son clowned into the mouth of a cannon on the Vicksburg battlefield; we all cheered for the corn-pone hero and threw peanuts at the villain aboard the showboat *Sprague*. Incidentally, storywise, we sailed down the Mississippi.

The experience was a tremendous eye-opener. The river, whose level varies on average over fifty feet a year, was in full spring spate. Even at our engine maximum of 4.5 knots, we were occasionally passed by logs not fifty feet away in the swirling current. At last I understood how lesser talents had won the Bermuda Race. In my pre-cruise imagination, I'd seen the Mississippi as "waitin' on the levee," scraping past towheads and snags, reading the bottom from moonlight on the riffles, and in general, Mark Twain's initiation as a pilot as revealed in *Life on the Mississippi*. But there were few towns, the levees were three to ten miles inshore, and there were few landings. Mainly we saw miles of scrub forest up to its armpits in Old Muddy. Except for the push-boats with their barges, and the occasional oil derrick, pecking away forlornly like some ante-diluvian crane, the Mississippi was largely deserted.

Natchez, surrounded by the antebellum mansions of cotton brokers, slumbered gently on its bluff; across from Baton Rouge, cane field hands' cabins were papered with generations of newsprint, which we peeled back to the 1870s. Our most dramatic adventure was running Ten Mile Cut in the black pitch of a moonless night. The night was windless, and the current was with us at better than our top speed. The river was forty-seven feet above low water. Halfway through the Cut, a pushboat with wall-to-wall barges fingered us with its two-mile search-light. I revved up the engine to its full 4.5 knots and rammed us into the starboard shrubbery until the mast tangled in the branches; the barges throbbed clear of our stern by several feet, and as their wake heaved us deeper, leaves and twigs rained on deck. In the burgeoning postpartum silence, my bride commented, "Mark Twain! Huh!"

The river's contents had recently melted in Canada and Minnesota, and I got the boat back into the mainstream by going over-board, standing on the random tree limb, and pushing. Thereafter, blue to the bellybutton and congealed to the nipples, I foreswore night adventure. The Mississippi had, however, opened my at-sea eyes to the shore and other lives upon it, and come the four months of summer, we were ready to expand the boat's potential.

We first trailered west to California's delta region, unique in the world. Above San Francisco, tract after tract has been recovered from vast marshes formed where the San Joaquin, Sacramento, and Moke-lumne rivers pour millions of gallons behind the coastal range. Mucked out, diked by their own dredgings, and pumped down to alluvial fecun-dity, fifteen feet below river level and five thousand acres at a time, the tracts grow onions, celery, tomatoes, carrots, and as an interim crop, "gyp corn." Then as you sail beyond the swampland and penetrate

I washed boat, trailer, and car every time the sun shone again.

California, the lion-colored hills rise in the sun's glare with their black-green trees and thousands of red cattle, fattening. Our boat drew a foot, bilgeboards up, her mast folded down with little effort. We ducked under bridges, slid into deserted pools among the tule reeds, docked at Grindstone Joe's, and visited backwater towns with drowsy Victorian waterfronts. Deep in a swamp, my son, aged twelve, found a Digger Indian burial ground and appropriated a skull. It took days to persuade him it was unappetizing, and to rebury it.

Our rhythm slowed, and we began to sail for pleasure, to explore to saturation. We trailered to Puget Sound, where the wind is at ease for most of the summer, and drifted around the San Juans, up to Nanaimo, to Vancouver, through hazy mornings and the light onshore breezes of afternoons, breathing salt air and sharp pine, tying to log-boom docks, cooking in the steak-smell of other voyagers, drinking and boasting with laughing fellow rovers. We rose late, stopped earlier and more often, and wandered deeper into the landscape and the ways of the locals.

We took a week to get in and out of Princess Louisa Inlet, sailing magnificently into the higher and tighter walls of Jervis Inlet's fjord, spinnaker set and the wind following on the same jibe around thirty-degree corners. The prodigality of the Northwest astonished the New Englander in me, massive mountains with snow peaks, virgin forests, deserted log cabins on sand bars stacked with a wealth of castaway logs, scene after scene unchanged from the crude sketches of George Vancouver's exploration.

The Atalanta summer became a better and better memory with the passage of time, and it helped me decide we'd retire into a life of cruising. Kitty and I have done almost exactly that for the last ten years. With now and then one of the children, and with a host of friends, we've cruised to Ireland, down to Spain, the length of the Mediterranean to the Greek Islands and up the Dalmatian Coast, back around Italy, over to Africa's north coast, back to Gibraltar, on to the Canaries, Antigua, Roatan, Mexico, and finally back to New England. We've circumnavigated New England, cruised the Maritimes, the Dutch Canals, the Crinan, the Caledonian, the Göta, the Panama, and the Kiel.

Guests make the trip a party. Just as visitors to your home town lead

At a Digger Indian burial ground, my son appropriated a skull.

F.O.B. and Wm. B. Hoyt II at Chatterbox Falls, Princess Louisa Inlet.

you to reexamine it, so shipmates introduce new patterns, new inter-
ests, new conversations. My drive to sail farther and faster has nudged
me into reading local history and related novels, attending local sports
events, visiting local industry, and trying local cuisine. Gradually, gradually, I've stopped putting up light sails at the whisper of opportunity.
Our "three-knot rule" for starting the engine has eased into a "four-
knot rule," and at the same time the seven-foot draft on *Telltale*, our
forty-one-foot sloop, has begun to seem restrictive. All those beckoning
thin waters grow more inviting as harbors get crowded and marina
charges escalate.

I suppose my trigger has been the Intracoastal Waterway. Sandy
beaches, islands of palm or pine, deserted coves, shores and inlets
teeming with birds—all these made me yearn for a boat whose draft
I could push off a beach without wetting my knees, whose momentum
I could stop with an outstretched foot, whose sails would disappear at
will, whose masts would fold for bridges and forests, whose propeller
would be housed against danger, whose engine could out-thrust rivers
and could run for drops of fuel and, what the hell, a boat whose
personality was as incorruptible as Herbert Hoover. In short, a shippa-
ble, trailerable, versatile gunk holer!

Actually, what years of sailing had been teaching me has finally
penetrated my consciousness. Racing, cruising, exploring, or passagemaking—what you do with any boat is to exploit its full potential
and let it explore yours. Boats, mainly marinaed and used to day sail
or for the weekend race, harbor the dreams of a wider life. Boats
planned are subconscious expressions of lives replanned, experience
expanded. Infinitely more than a house, a boat is a machine for living
at peak. In our own *Telltale* we have the ideal offshore cruiser (for us);
what must our inshore boat be? What form, what functions, what will
we do with it?

First, we'd like to circumnavigate the eastern United States—up
the Hudson, out the Erie Canal, through the Trent-Severn Waterway
to the Great Lakes, and down the length of the Mississippi, until we
got to the ins and outs of the bayous and backwaters of the Gulf Coast.
We'd like to wander homewards up the Intracoastal Waterway, to trail
to the Ohio and the Tennessee-Tombigbee. Would it be possible, 100

Our two-boat navy's second boat.

years after Thoreau, to spend two weeks on the Concord and Merrimac Rivers, listening to a considerably different drummer? There are over 16,000 miles of navigable rivers and canals in the United States alone, and as I add them up in the *Guinness Guide to the Waterways of Europe*, 15,418 miles of navigable waterways in Europe: 279 in Belgium, 889 in Sweden, 949 in the British Isles, 4,094 in Germany, 4,600 in Holland, and 4,607 in France.

We could ship the boat to Europe and cruise for five or six years, then, since Japanese car carriers go home light, ship to Japan and explore the Inland Sea. And, at the last, as the shadows lengthen, and the evening comes, we'd return to the United States for our twilight years and, following the sun, wander the bays, sounds, and rivers from the Chesapeake to Brownsville, Texas.

So we needed a centerboard boat, twenty-six feet by eight feet (the maximum for trailering without special permits) with an engine that could beat a quick river (or Ten Mile Cut) and modest weight. We chose a Walt Scott design, a Beachcomber cat-ketch, and named her *Anecdote* ("a brief tale, amusingly told"). Her roller furling and reefing masts, unstayed, allow us to set or furl both sails in under a minute; she draws eighteen inches minimum, and her twelve horsepower Yanmar moves her at six and a half knots, cruising, for just over a quart of diesel an hour.

So now we have a two-boat navy, ready for any eventuality. It hasn't resolved our inconsistencies, however it gratifies both offshore and sheltered water yearnings. Now I know that in my gray years we'll still be sailing, surrounded by land sheltering water, as I did in that first sailing summer of my youth. Just the other day I read of F. B. Cooke, British author of *The Singlehanded Yachtsman*, himself a tireless explorer of every estuary, river, canal, creek, and tidehole in southern England. Retiring at middle age (70), he pursued his addiction aboard a succession of tiny craft until his death at 102! By such standards, Kitty and I have 35 percent of our lives to live, and 80 percent of navigable inland waters still to explore, sheltered from gales, and certain of cruising company.